PMP Exam Prep

Simplified

Essential Tactics to Ace the Project Management Professional Exam on Your First Try

Victoria Pembroke

TABLE OF CONTENTS

INTRODUCTION

My siblings and cousins are all highly successful—I'm talking doctors and lawyers. As I'm one of the younger members of our generation, I was *eventually* asked what I wanted to be when I grew up. I knew what I wanted—birthing, organizing, and running events and other ideas were always my greatest joy. I smiled and said, "A project manager."

Lifted eyebrows and funny glances occasionally came my way. One of my cousins, who happens to be a highly successful businessman, cautioned me: "Do you even know what that is? Do you think you have what it takes?" I simply responded with, "I'll learn." And I did!

While I was still on my way to becoming a project manager, I was part of a project handled by six teams under one main contractor. The different teams specialized in the various areas relating to the project. Of course, we had a project manager. Let's call him Gordon. I had such admiration for him. He always seemed calm and collected, never rude, but passionate and determined. He was my role model. I wanted to be like him one day.

We ran into a snag, but I'll keep it short. We had no way of determining the number of hours worked by every member of each team. So, Gordon called a meeting. He asked the IT and tech guys to write a program that could be used to determine our worked hours. Every member of each team would clock in and out of this system, which would automatically calculate the number of hours worked per day, week, month, and so forth. Great idea, right?

The program was created with tremendous success. However, it took some time for people to get used to it. And guess who was in charge of the system? Yes, that's right. Me.

When I reminded team members to clock in, I was accused of being bossy and told to "mind my own business." I felt I had no other choice but to talk to Gordon. He called a meeting once more, and instead of ripping off heads, he calmly explained why the system was so important. Ultimately, it determined how many collective hours were worked and even pinpointed where some teams could be overworked. Beautifully done! It worked! Except for one senior team member (who wasn't on my company's team).

He kept on giving me a hard time. He would even coerce his team members not to use the clock-in system simply to give me a hard time. Since I had already discussed this with my team's project manager, I felt I couldn't do it again. I didn't want to be labeled by the other team members. However, Gordon was thorough. He came to me and said, "I noticed that some people are still not using the system. I think I know why. Don't worry about it."

That's all he said. He left and arranged a meeting with the hard-headed team. One meeting—that's *all* it took. Everyone complied afterward. The mentioned senior team member was friendly and cooperative for the remainder of the project. I don't know what happened in that meeting, but whatever it was, it worked. As I observed Gordon, I knew what he had that made a difference: He had authority. It was undeniable and strong, rooted in his passion for planning and executing. That's who I wanted to be. Being a project manager wasn't simply about having a higher salary—it was about doing what I loved and doing it with passion, authority, and courage.

I won't lie; being a project manager means facing countless challenges and pitfalls. Most projects are like temples. You have to maneuver like you're Lara Croft. But, before you get there, there's the PMP exam. About this, I won't lie either— it's tough. Even so, it is possible to pass. Remember that what you put in is what you'll get out. You won't be offered a free or even cheap ride to get through it. It will take hard work and thorough preparation.

To be successful, you need to have a fire in your soul. Are you passionate about becoming a project manager? Do you desperately want it? Do you believe you have what it takes? If your answer is yes, then roar like a lion! Be brave and bold. You can do this!

You're not alone, either. I'll be with you. Together, we'll look at the PMP exam, its style and format, and also some strategies for preparing for the exam. We'll explore the aspects of a project, such as integration, scope, quality, and cost. Furthermore, we'll discuss communication and stakeholder management. We'll talk about how you can be prepared for the big day, and you'll find some practice questions and mock exams.

You'll be given examples and helpful tips to help you apply what you learn in the real world. Perhaps you can find a mentor, someone you can look up to like I did with Gordon.

Yes, the road ahead will take a lot of effort. And it won't be easy. But then again, what is truly worth it if it doesn't come with a bit of a challenge?

CHAPTER 1:

THE PMP EXAM

So, you plan on taking the Project Management Professional (PMP) exam. The question is—how hard can it be? Don't expect to be memorizing a ton of knowledge so you can answer questions quickly in the exam. The exam does not simply test your memory of facts but your capability of applying the knowledge and techniques you've gained to real-world scenarios.

This means that you'll focus on the PMP framework and guidelines rather than trying to memorize questions. These will help you answer the questions presented in the exam. Furthermore, if you have a lot of experience in project management, you may find the exams somewhat less challenging than people with less experience.

If you feel like you don't have enough experience, don't fret. It only means that you'll have to study a bit harder. If possible, try to get some more experience with managing projects. Once you have the knowledge and can apply it to related scenarios, you should feel more confident about passing this exam.

What You Need to Know

There has been a rise in people wanting to take the PMP exam, and with good reason. According to the Project Management Institute (PMI), there's a 10-year faster demand growth for project managers than for people in any other field (PMI, 2017). This means there aren't enough professionally skilled project managers to fill this gap.

The best way to become professionally skilled is to become certified by taking (and passing) the PMP exam. The exam is a computer-based test (CBT) of tasks and multiple-choice questions designed to test your knowledge of project management principles and concepts.

But why is this certification so important? Once you have it, it proves that you are a skilled and professional project manager who can manage and lead projects in any industry and for any company. Let me tell you, when you have passed this exam, you certainly deserve your spot that high on the corporate ladder.

Perhaps you wonder if anyone can apply for and take the PMP exam. The answer is "no." There are some requirements, which are:

- You must have a four-year degree or equivalent.

- You must complete 35 hours of project management

education.

- You must have at least three years of project management experience.

The fantastic thing is that your PMP credential is recognized globally. Also, there are testing centers worldwide where you can take the exam. The certification proves you can manage and lead projects in any company or field, and you can do so in any city or country! This certification will make you stand out above other applicants whenever an organization is looking to hire new project managers.

Your mental state plays a big part in whether you'll pass the exam. Sure, it's normal to be nervous, but if you keep feeding yourself negative thoughts, you seriously jeopardize your chances of succeeding. So, get rid of thoughts such as *it will be too difficult!* or *I don't know if I'm good enough*. If you're afraid you won't be sufficiently prepared for the exam, good! Because *then* you can do something about it! You have a chance to prepare well. You'll feel confident in your abilities when you pass and get that certification.

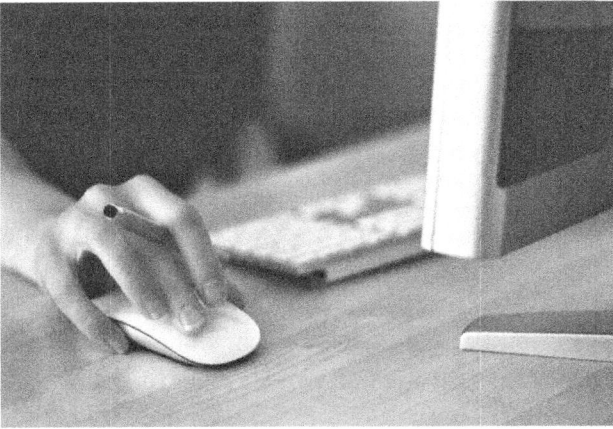

There are many project managers out there who like to meet like-minded people. With this certification, you can network with other project manager professionals. You'll engage in small talk and exchange tactics, techniques, creative ideas, and strategies. You'll have the opportunity to make a significant change in your organization. *And* it will allow you to negotiate an appropriate pay raise or promotion.

Globally, project manager professionals earn a salary of 16% higher than non-certified professionals. In America, PMI-certified managers make 32% more than other managers in their respective fields (PMI, 2023).

I am sure that, just like I did, you don't want to go into the PMP exam blindly. You want to know what it will be like, right?

In the exam, you'll find tasks and multiple-choice questions based on the Project Management Institute's PMBOK guide. You'll notice four sections: initiating, planning, executing, and monitoring and controlling. Each section has a different number of questions and weighting.

The weighting is divided as follows: initiation is 13%, planning is 23%, executing is 30%, and monitoring and controlling is 34%. Once you have finished a section, you can't return to it; you must complete each section in the specified timeframe. Does this give you a better understanding of why preparing effectively is vital before attempting this exam?

Each section will be scored according to its weighting, meaning you'll have to pass each section independently. Furthermore, you'll need an overall score of at least 61% to pass the PMP exam.

If you are serious about being a project management professional, prepare well enough to pass the PMP exam on your first try. However, if you do not pass, you can retake the exam after a month. You have an eligibility period of 12 months in which you can retake the exam up to three times. There are testing centers worldwide where you can take the exam or use a proctored service to take the exam online.

Yes, the PMP exam *is* challenging. But you *can* pass it on your first try by being fully prepared. Many project managers fail on their first attempt because they haven't prepared properly. One way to significantly increase your chance of passing is by using PMP exam prep courses.

Since the exam is based on the PMBOK guide, we should examine what it is, its purpose, and why it is a project manager's guide.

Preface to the PMBOK Manual

The global project management industry considers the Project Management Body of Knowledge (PMBOK) as a complete set of guidelines on practices, procedures, and terminologies for any company and project management professional. Organizations find PMBOK valuable, as it allows them to avoid project failure by standardizing procedures across different divisions and altering procedures to meet particular requirements.

The body of knowledge must be updated and circulated often as it expands continually with new techniques or best practices discovered by professional project managers. The PMI, a nonprofit member association of project management professionals, monitors this initiative.

Although PMBOK is more of an industry framework for best practices in project management than a methodology, it is frequently associated with the "waterfall methodology" which aligns project stages sequentially. Agile, one of the more recent methodologies, is also compatible with PMBOK.

The PMI does not promote any specific methodology since PMBOK procedures can be adjusted to fit various project management scenarios. Instead, project managers choose the procedures that are best suited for their organization, teams, and projects.

The Origins of PMBOK

Back in 1969, the PMI was established by project managers who wanted a place to exchange information and discuss issues relating to project management. The first certification offered by the PMI was the PMP certification in 1984. 1987 a PMBOK white paper was published, followed by the PMBOK Guide's exposure draft in 1994 ("What is PMBOK," 2023).

The PMBOK Guide

The Guide to the Project Management Body of Knowledge (PMBOK Guide) was first published by the PMI in 1996. Its seventh edition was released in 2021 and is available in 12 languages. Simply put, it is an instructional book for professionals in managing various projects. It provides them with terminology, fundamental standards, and directives relating to project management.

However, remember that the PMBOK Guide's seventh edition does *not* replace the sixth edition. Managers looking for a process-based approach will still use the sixth edition, while managers who prefer a principles-based approach will find the seventh edition very handy. In the past, the newer editions replaced the previous ones, but not in this instance. Instead of a replacement, the seventh edition is an extension of information available in the sixth edition.

Technology develops at an incredible rate and is used by most organizations. Therefore, it makes sense that the PMBOK Guide should be updated accordingly. New technology means companies find fresh ways of doing things, leading to fast market changes.

Updated areas in the PMBOK Guide include the following:

- The manual uses PMI standards to provide further direction on implementing the PMBOK Guide in real-life situations.

- It features a whole section devoted to customizing strategy and procedures.

- The manual focuses not just on deliverables but also on project results.

- It covers all development methodologies: traditional, agile, adaptive, predictive, and hybrid.

- You'll find a "Models, Methods, and Artifacts" section and a longer list of techniques and tools.

In short, the PMBOK Guide was updated to adapt to changes in the global industry, which means it will be helpful and effective in helping project managers set, pursue, and achieve their goals.

I know you have a lot to digest. Take some deep breaths, calm your mind, and *then* we'll delve into the critical knowledge areas and process groups.

Key Knowledge Areas and Process Groups

In this section, we'll explore the knowledge areas and process groups that are essential for project success. Get to know them well—they are the backbone of project management.

The Knowledge Areas

There are 10 PMP knowledge areas to be learned and understood, as these will play a big part in helping you pass the PMP exam; however, their importance goes beyond that. The knowledge areas effectively promote success in project planning and execution and will help you become a proficient project manager overall.

Project Integration Management

Consider this to be your project's overall view. This broad category includes all the steps and tasks necessary to complete the project, tying everything together from its beginning to its conclusion. Furthermore, this area allows you to weigh the project against your company's missions, visions, and goals. Is the project aligned with these? Don't forget about the stakeholders—their goals must also be considered.

Project Scope Management

The scope is the framework of the project and aims to ensure the project's success. Finalizing all the components and delivering the outcomes as scheduled rely on a defined, validated, and controlled scope. Adhering to the scope and setting relevant expectations prevent unrelated tasks from interfering with the project. The knowledge about this area will help you and everyone else involved remain focused on the project.

Project Schedule Management

As a project manager, you'll need to manage the schedules and timelines of every team member. This knowledge area makes that possible. Not only will you establish a timeline for the project, but you will also instruct your team members on what to do and when. Schedule management also means thinking and planning ahead of time and preparing yourself for any issues that may arise. This includes possible changes that must be made, ensuring the project will be completed on time.

Project Cost Management

Your project will obligate expectations, but they must align with reality. You'll have to set up a budget and then oversee and manage it to achieve this. This will also help you keep track of labor, materials, resources, and any other costs that may be involved.

Project Quality Management

This knowledge area covers end-to-end quality assurance, control, and requirements. How else would you define the value standards in a project, let alone meet them? Again, you'll need to plan for any issues concerning the quality of the deliverables. It should be in line with the project's schedule and budget costs.

Project Resource Management

Resources need to be managed throughout the duration of the project. Tools, supplies, materials, and team members are all examples of project resources. The success of the project relies greatly on these. It includes accurately estimating, planning, acquiring, developing, managing, and controlling all project resources.

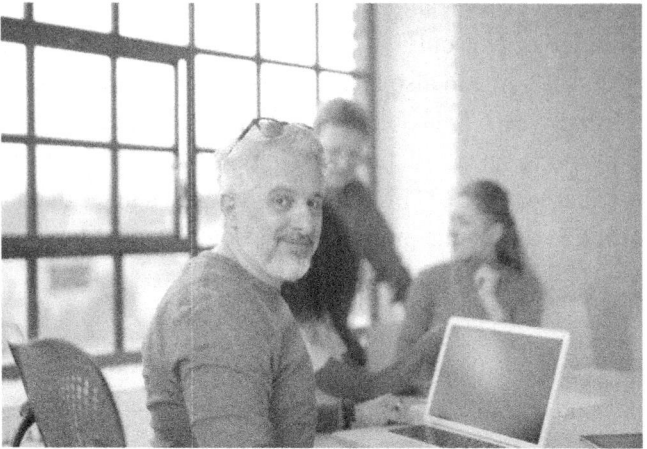

Project Communications Management

Never underestimate the importance of effective communication. Adhering to this knowledge area includes keeping stakeholders up to date, managing and monitoring all communication related to the project, and ensuring crisp communication among team members. However, you must first determine the project's communication needs. Doing this lets you rest more easily, knowing everything is going according to plan.

Project Risk Management

The bigger the project, the more risks may be involved. Planning with these risks in mind will help you keep your project on course, even if some of these risks materialize. By utilizing this knowledge area, you'll cover risk prioritization, planned responses, regulating and monitoring risk levels, and risk identification through qualitative and quantitative risk analysis.

Project Procurement Management

This knowledge area is essential if your project requires outside resources, such as vendors, contractors, or any other resource that needs to be hired. You'll have to identify, hire, manage, and monitor all outside resources with your project's budget in mind.

Project Stakeholder Management

Every project is born to meet the demands of an individual or group—the stakeholders. You'll have to get to know them, listen to their issues or suggestions, effectively manage their expectations, meet their requirements, and communicate with them successfully. As their dreams originated the project, they are vital to its success. Handle with care!

After its latest update, the PMP exam has shifted its focus to three domains: People, Process, and Business Environment. However, this does not imply that the critical knowledge areas and process groups have vanished. They simply exist as a subset of the three domains.

Although the knowledge areas and process groups mainly belong to the Process domain, they are represented in all three domains. You'll better understand the natural flow of a project and its relevant principles and processes by understanding the critical knowledge areas and process groups. It will enable you to identify the proper documentation, tools, and approaches to handle a range of disputes and circumstances.

The Process Groups

The five PMP process groups—Initiating, Planning, Executing, Monitoring and Controlling, and Closing—constitute the project lifecycle. The knowledge areas are closely tied to the tasks under the new domains and are mapped to the five process groups. To make it a bit easier to understand, the Project Management Academy has a great graphic, prepared by Erin Aldridge, outlining the key knowledge areas, the five process groups, and the activities related to them, found here at https://projectmanagementacademy.net/resources/blog/understanding-pmp-knowledge-areas-for-the-pmp-exam/ (Aldridge, 2021).

When you understand how the different aspects of project management relate to each other and align with the domains, namely People, Process, and Business Environment, it will be easier to identify the required resources and when to use them. Memorizing all this information can help, but in the end, you must effectively apply domains, enablers, tools, and tasks to the situations you'll find in the PMP exam.

You may feel worried or even overwhelmed because of the significant changes in the PMP exam. Remember, it will still test your ability to be an efficient project manager; your knowledge and practices will be tested.

The updates to the exam cater to a broader range of project management skills and approaches. The knowledge areas may not be as prominent as before, but you still need a clear understanding of them and the process groups to increase your chances of passing the exam on your first try.

Again, don't simply try to memorize all the information—make it a part of your practice. Understand it and think more about how the information can be implemented in real-world scenarios. This is why actual experience is so valuable. You can apply what you find in the PMBOK Guide to your projects.

Knowing more about the PMP exam's format and style will help you better prepare. Therefore, we'll cover that in the next chapter, as well as how to apply for the exam and what you need to be eligible.

CHAPTER 2:

FORMAT AND STYLE OF
THE PMP EXAM

Now that we've laid the foundation for what you need to know (and be skilled at), we'll look at what the PMP exam will look like. We'll also discuss how to apply for the exam and all the aspects that will ensure your eligibility. So, calm your mind, see this as an adventure, and then we'll continue.

Format and Style of the PMP Exam

The exam lasts 230 minutes, and you'll have to answer 180 questions. Five of these questions do not count toward the final score and are used to determine, according to their results, whether they will be considered for future PMP exams. This means 175 of the 180 questions will count toward your final mark. However, don't try to guess which questions do not count, as they are spread randomly throughout the exam. It's vital that you answer every question—don't skip anything!

The scoring will depend on the weighting of the section. The questions will test your ability to utilize project management techniques and principles, including risk management, planning and organizing, procurement management, and monitoring and controlling.

Also, remember that once you've completed a section and moved on, you can't go back to those questions. So, make sure that you answer everything before moving on.

You'll have the option of taking two 10-minute breaks. Some people prefer pushing through, but I recommend taking these breaks. The exam is tough and tiring. You'll need the rest, even if only for a few minutes. It will allow you to calm down, clear your mind, and regain your focus.

Domains

Previously, the PMP exams focused on the ten knowledge areas and five process groups. These are still an integral part of the exam, but after the update, the exam now focuses on three domains: people, processes, and business environment.

- **People**: This domain will test your ability to lead as a project manager.

- **Process**: In this domain, your technical skills related to project management will be tested.

- **Business Environment**: This domain is all about, well, business. It will test your skills to handle organizational change management, business acumen, and compliance.

Things You'll Likely Encounter

There are many different things you may encounter in the PMP exam. Let's talk about some of them.

Questions Related to Processes

These questions are important and apply to many aspects of project management. You may be expected to rearrange processes correctly, fill in missing parts, or know what happens after specific processes.

Fantastical Facts

Yes, you may be presented with questions or statements that contain purely made-up terms. They are designed to throw you off. Pay close attention and identify them. You may even encounter paragraphs of erroneous information. The only way to get past this is to be well-informed!

Situational Scenes

When you sit down to start your exam, you must take on the role of a project management professional. You may be asked how to initiate or close a project. You'll be presented with many situations and must use your professional savvy and skills to answer and solve them. So, when you start the exam, don't think like a candidate—think like the masterful project management professional you aim to be.

Next, we'll cover different questions you'll find in the exam. Relax, be calm, and continue.

Question Types

PMI decided to include a broader range of question types other than the traditional multiple-choice questions. These include drag-and-drop type questions, fill-in-the-blanks, and hot spots.

Multiple-Choice

With these questions, you'll be given a statement or question with four possible answers. Only one will be correct, while the other three are distractors (incorrect answers). The distractors are usually challenging to distinguish. They often seem close to being correct but aren't. Keep in mind that while two or even three answers may appear to be right, you have to choose the one that is the best answer for the specific question or scenario.

If you are sure about the answers to some questions, answer them immediately, but you must be completely confident. You have a limited time, but still, don't rush it! Skip those questions you're unsure about for the moment. However, don't move on to the next section before you have answered *all* the questions in the current section.

After answering everything you are sure of, go back to those you had doubts about. Begin by eliminating some of the distractors. If you eliminate at least two of them, you already have a 50/50 chance of getting the correct answer.

Multiple-Response

You'll be given possible answers to these questions, of which you'll have to pick more than one answer. Some of these questions will have more than four possibilities. Remember, *always* choose the best answer.

The questions can be tricky. They are presented in a way that requires you to consider all the information provided to choose the correct answers. A few of them may have obvious answers, but you'll find most of them challenging. As you pick an option, think about how they would work together with your other chosen answers. Ultimately, your chosen answers must all work together to address the situation. Stay calm and keep your focus.

Hot Spot

You will be presented with a graph or diagram, and questions will be asked about it. You'll have to click on the diagram or graph to pinpoint the solution to the question. Sometimes, you'll have to click on more than one area. Think calmly about the question because you'll have to click on the correct and relevant area to the situation or scenario depicted in the question.

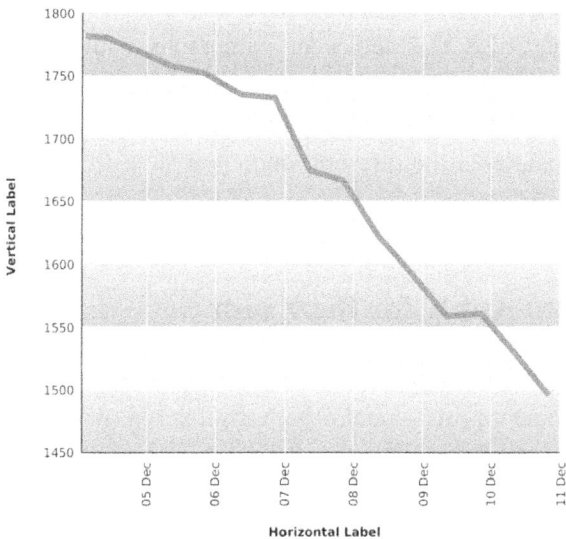

Vertical Label (y-axis): 1450, 1500, 1550, 1600, 1650, 1700, 1750, 1800

Horizontal Label (x-axis): 05 Dec, 06 Dec, 07 Dec, 08 Dec, 09 Dec, 10 Dec, 11 Dec

Drag-and-Drop

You'll find several items that need rearranging, which you can do by dragging and dropping them in the correct order. For instance, you may be given various descriptions of project phases, and you'll have to drag and drop them in the correct sequence to represent a project's life cycle.

You'll have to rearrange information correctly or chronologically. Also, you may be given definitions that you'll have to drag to their correct terms or vice versa.

Fill-In-The-Blanks

You may find this type of question throughout the exam. For instance, when you answer multiple-choice or multiple-response questions, parts of the presented scenario may be omitted to be filled by your choice or choices.

You may also find tables or paragraphs with blanked-out spaces that need filling. In such cases, you'll find a box where you can enter the missing information. This means you have only completed the question once you have filled in all the blanks.

How to Apply for the Exam

When I first wanted to be certified and become a project management professional, I honestly felt overwhelmed by all the information, similar to what you've encountered up until now. It made me feel nervous and a bit scared. Okay, a *lot* scared. But, after speaking with my learning consultant, I decided to do as he suggested—instead of seeing all this as intimidating, I saw it as an exciting journey. I turned it into an adventure.

Can you do the same? Think about it—this is your chance to become what you've dreamed about. Don't let anything or anyone stand in your way. Be confident and trust in your skills.

And how do you know you're applying for the correct PMP certification? The organization you're using to apply must be affiliated with PMI. Make sure that they are!

After thorough preparation, you'll be ready to apply for the exam. Let's discuss the steps required to do that.

It Takes Three Steps

Yes, it only takes three steps to apply for the PMP exam. These steps are necessary for you to showcase your experience and training. You have to prove that you've got what it requires to become a certified project management professional.

Step One: Confirming Your Eligibility

Here, you'll gather information to provide the PMI that details your educational and in-job experience. You'll also mention any other project management training you have completed.

To be eligible, you must have a four-year degree or equivalent, complete 35 hours of project management education, and have at least three years of project management experience.

Step Two: Gather Your Information

In this step, you'll gather the details of your education, training, and project management experience. For your education, make sure your supporting documents include the institution's name, the years you attended, your field of study, the country in which you studied, and the highest level you have achieved.

For the training details, you'll name the institutions that you've attended, the details of the courses you've completed, when you have completed them, and how many qualifying hours you have under your belt.

For the project management details, you'll name the organizations where you've led projects and give details about your role, what you were responsible for, and the timeframes of the projects you've managed.

Step Three: Completing and Submitting Your Application

To complete the final step, you must have an account with PMI. This can be set up when you register with them or apply for the PMP exam. To make the application easier, ensure you have all the information you've gathered in steps one and two. If you cannot complete the application due to unforeseen circumstances, don't worry. You can save your progress and continue at a later time.

You don't have to be a member of the PMI to apply for the exam. PMI membership does cost $129 per year (as of 2023), but it's well worth it. You'll have access to the salary report, electronic versions of the PMBOK Guide, and other standards and guides that PMI has published. You can also join a local chapter, which will cost a small yearly fee. However, you don't need to belong to a local chapter to be a PMI member.

So, You've Applied—What Comes Next?

Your information will be checked for your eligibility to be verified. Once it is verified, your application will be accepted. Then, you can make a payment toward your exam fee. As of 2023, the fee for PMI members is $405, and for non-members, it is $555.

Take note that the PMI can select random candidates to audit their eligibility. If you are picked for an audit, provide them with a copy of your degree, details of your experience validated by your supervisor or manager's signature, and a certificate proving you have at least 35 hours of project management training.

Once you have paid your fees, you can schedule when you'll be taking the PMP exam. You can either take the exam at a testing center or securely online. It must be mentioned that if you don't pass, you can retake the test up to three times in one year.

Eligibility Requirements and Supporting Documents

You must have all your details ready and complete your application form accurately. If not, you may be rejected as a candidate, or time will needlessly be wasted before you are considered as a candidate. Besides, knowing how to organize your information and completing the application thoroughly will give them a preview of your organizational and cognitive skills. First impressions last!

So, to make more sense of what will be required of you, let's discuss the details regarding your eligibility requirements and the supporting documents you'll need when you apply.

No Lightweight Standards

PMI has set high standards for anyone aspiring project management professional. This is already evident when you apply for the PMP exam. But think about it: When a company hires a person with the PMP certification, they expect someone more than efficient at managing projects. With the high standards, PMI virtually guarantees any organization that they will get the person they need, as long as the said person has the PMP certification.

Also, on average, project managers with the certification receive a higher salary than their non-certified peers. This means you must be worth every cent you're paid.

So, before you are even considered a candidate for the exam, PMI will investigate your eligibility. Your educational requirements prove that you have sufficient theoretical background to effectively manage projects, while the required experience proves that you have the basic skills to attempt the exam. But remember—your experience will, in turn, affect your educational requirements.

When an organization sees that you are a certified PMP, they'll automatically bank on your excellent knowledge and skills in project management. Why? Because they know about the high standards set by PMI, especially with the education and experience requirements before the exam is taken.

Education

The first set of criteria involves you having a bachelor's degree or equivalent experience, as just having a high school diploma isn't enough by itself. The requirements are determined by the education you have.

Bachelor's Degree

If you have a bachelor's degree or a global equivalent, you must have at least 36 months (three years) of experience in project management. You must have spent at least 4,500 hours leading and directing projects during these three years. Lastly, you must have completed at least 35 hours of education in project management.

High School Diploma

If you don't have a bachelor's degree but have a high school diploma or a global equivalent, you will need at least 60 months (five years) of project management experience. You must have spent 7,500 hours in these 60 months leading and directing projects. In this case, you'll also be required to have spent at least 35 hours in project management education.

You may be eligible to take the PMP exam if you match these two educational requirements. If you are unsure how to obtain the 35 hours of project management education, you can enroll in PMP certification training to get the required education and reinforce your likelihood of candidacy.

As a bonus, enrolling in this training dramatically improves your chance of passing the exam on your first try. The trainers are experts and will support your endeavor while helping you significantly improve your skills.

Experience

Do you remember the five process groups we discussed in Chapter 1? The experience you've provided in your application must span across all five groups. This is required as these groups are standards set by the PMI and appear in the PMBOK Guide. The good news is that they needn't all be covered in every single project as long as all of your project management experience combined involves the five process groups.

Here are some examples of acceptable project-based tasks:

- To ensure that their business needs were in harmony with the project alignment, you obtained feedback by discussing the project status with the stakeholders.

- Whenever necessary, you presented the project plan to the key stakeholders to get their consent to proceed.

- To meet the project goals set by the client, you determined the project's high-level scope based on business needs and compliance.

- Your team completed the deliverables on time and within the designated budget by carrying out the actions outlined in the project plan.

- To ensure that the project's scope and deliverables were satisfied, you collaborated with the client and the sponsor to gain final acceptance of the project deliverables.

Can you see how the five process groups are associated with these points?

Remember that if you have a bachelor's degree or a global equivalent, you must have at least three years of experience leading projects totaling at least 4,500 hours. Should you have a high school diploma or a global equivalent, it changes to five years of at least 7,500 hours of managing projects.

PMI is not kidding with their standards! The requirements are high, but how else can organizations be confident they will get what they need?

If you don't have the required hours of experience yet, you can work toward getting them. Should you be a full-time project manager, just keep on going until you have accumulated the required hours.

If you're not a full-time project manager, there are some things you can do to help. Start by changing your role. Advertise yourself. Let your organization know how valuable and skilled you are. Don't shy away in a corner. Be confident in your abilities and show them what you can do. Tell them that you want to develop your career by being of more value to the company, namely by managing projects.

Perhaps the organization you're working for is unwilling to provide you with the needed opportunities. If so, look for one that will. Spread your wings and make yourself known. If organizations don't know about you, how will they hire you? You'll be surprised how many people in management positions are willing to negotiate terms and conditions as long as they have certainty in your ability to deliver.

Some organizations are looking for aspiring project managers willing to volunteer to take on projects. This can be a last resort to get the hours you need to apply for the exam. Besides, you've only got a lot to gain. Belonging to a PMI chapter can help, as they can point you in the right direction. This is also a fantastic way to build your network and support system.

Now that you know about the structure of the PMP exam and all the requirements you must meet to apply to take the exam, you'll want to start preparing—that is, if you met all the requirements and were able to apply.

I'm sure you have excellent skills in project management, but how are your studying skills? In the next chapter, we'll cover exam preparation, and you'll find advice on developing an effective study plan. As mentioned, studying for the PMP exam does not mean you'll simply have to memorize facts. You have to understand these facts and be able to apply them in real-world scenarios.

Like I always say, knowledge is gained from learning, and wisdom is applying that knowledge.

CHAPTER 3:

EXAM PREPARATION STRATEGIES

Just because you may be a skilled project manager does not mean you can simply jump right into the PMP exam. You must be well-prepared; by that, I'm referring to studying. This exam is tricky because you can't just memorize facts to pass—you must be able to apply these facts and theories in real-life scenarios.

So, to get optimal results, you must study effectively. In this chapter, we'll talk about exam preparation strategies, how to develop a study plan and timeline that will benefit you most, and how to spend your physical and mental energy in a way that will result in zero wastefulness.

It's Crunch Time!

Since there's an increasing demand for certified project managers (and there will be for several years to come), you have a golden opportunity to prove yourself and jump a couple of steps up the corporate ladder. Be confident in your skills without being overconfident. Don't assume you won't have to "study as hard" as you're already killing it as a project manager.

Project management is vast—many different fields, methods, and applications exist. Even though you might be a genius in your field, you may only have touched the tip of the iceberg. You'll probably be pleasantly surprised by what you can still learn as you study. You'll also have to envision applying these things to real scenarios. That's what will be expected of you while writing the PMP exam.

Strategies to Remember

You should keep some things in mind as you prepare to study.

Define Your Why

Before you think of applying, ask yourself why you want to have the title of project management professional. After you have applied, you will be investing money, time, and other resources into preparing for the exam. Remember that you'll likely have to give up some things you enjoyed doing to make more time for studying. You may have to skip a few weeks or months of boys' night on Fridays or girls' night out on Tuesdays. Are you willing to do that? If so, why?

Can you answer that? Why is it so important to define your "why?" Because if you don't have a clear picture of why you want to do this, you'll likely lose interest and become demotivated. Your "why" may include wanting to expand your portfolio, change jobs, negotiate a pay raise, get a promotion, or switch industries altogether. All these are valid reasons, but are they enough to drive you to success?

My advice? Be motivated by who you are and the desire to become better at what you do—in other words, become an even more skilled project manager. Make it personal. Personal reasons tend to stick and keep us motivated.

Devise a Study Plan

Just thinking about taking the exam may already rev up your nerves. Having a study plan can help you reduce stress. Devise one that will consider your availability, primarily if you work full-time and have other responsibilities. However, don't use responsibilities as an excuse not to study. Delegate if you can, but do anything to increase your study time.

Your study plan should genuinely meet your needs. Be honest as you devise it, continually considering the bigger picture. Study as often as possible—there's no point in killing the goose that lays the golden egg, right?

Make a list of what you must do daily, including your studies, and stick to it. You'll be happy you did.

Learn From Smart People

If you haven't done so yet, join some PMP communities. I think it's safe to say that anyone who has ever taken the PMP exam understands the stresses you are experiencing. Some may even have experienced similar difficulties, such as unclear on some of the study material. If you feel stuck, ask around. Someone who has suffered the same can show you how they resolved the issue or explain what something means.

There are many PMP community platforms you can join. Use your search engine to find these platforms, such as projectmanagement.com or growacto.com.

The Pomodoro Technique

This technique may be especially useful if you feel overwhelmed. Study for 25 minutes, then take a five-minute break. You can set a timer to keep track. After four 25-minute sessions, take a longer break, between 15 to 30 minutes. By dividing the study load into chunks, you can easily digest the information.

However, since the exam is nearly four hours long and only offers two 10-minute breaks, you should eventually discipline yourself to stay focused longer. While the Pomodoro Technique can help you process information, don't get too used to only having to focus for a short while.

Set a Deadline

Perhaps you have decided to start studying before applying for the exam. I don't recommend doing that. First, you must apply to know if you are accepted to take the exam. PMI is strict, as you now know. You also understand why PMI's eligibility requirements and standards are set this high, right?

Don't attempt to tweak your eligibility requirements to succeed. If PMI discovers this (and they likely will), you'll lose this opportunity, and disciplinary action will be taken against you. If a person has tweaked their eligibility requirements and successfully becomes a candidate for the exam, they're not out of the woods. They may even have passed the exam, but the moment PMI discovers tweaked eligibility requirements, they'll strip that person of the title of project manager professional, and disciplinary steps can still be taken against them.

So, apply honestly and thoroughly, and if you're successful and are approved as a candidate, set your exam date. But set the date so you'll have enough time to study and prepare appropriately.

Secondly, you automatically have a deadline if you have an exam date. You'll better know how to plan your study time and how much you'd need to study every day.

Eating the Elephant

You may feel that you still have a long time before the exam, so there's enough time for partying and playing games. No, there isn't! Don't fall victim to "student syndrome." As soon as you've created your study plan, begin studying and stick to it! You'll only thank yourself in the end.

How do you eat an elephant? One bite at a time. But if you wait until the last moment, you'll never be able to digest the entire elephant in time—you'll choke! Don't procrastinate!

Practice, Practice, and More Practice

Use current questions in the PMP field and set up a PMP exam scenario for yourself. Answer the questions as if you're in the exam, using the same time frames, namely 230 minutes with two 10-minute breaks. The more you do it, the more you'll get used to it. You need to get to a point of "comfort" with the pressure and time frame. Set up your exam in the format discussed in Chapter 2, including the different question types.

Developing a Study Plan and Timeline

Let's face it: our lives are typically hectic, with little time to spare and study. But, with a fruitful study plan, you can gain sufficient learning to pass the PMP exam. In this section, we'll look at aspects you can work into your study plan to make studying more constructive and how to work around the time you have available.

It's All About Your Study Plan

First, we'll discuss what you can do to make studying effective and worthwhile.

Keep a Project-Based Mindset

You have the mindset of a project manager, right? Apply this trait to your exam preparations. See the preparations as a project and plan similarly, using your experience, expertise, and project management knowledge. Take the same steps: define the scope of your study materials; define your deliverables, which are the information you gain by studying; and stick to a schedule to complete your studies.

Use Material That Works for You

There's an ocean of study and reference material available. However, don't simply grab the first material you can access and use only that. Look around first. Find the material that will suit you best.

Larry, a friend, aspired to become a project management professional. His organization was ecstatic about it and sent him on PMP courses. His institution provided him with the PMBOK Guide, course material, and mock exams. He was successful in his studies, as shown by the results of the mock exams. So, the organization Larry worked for set him up for the PMP exam. Unfortunately, Larry was set up for failure.

He did not pass the PMP exam, as the questions were nothing like the ones he took in the mock exams. He was understandably frustrated. After picking himself up, he consulted with colleagues who were certified project management professionals. They gave him great advice and pointed him to other institutions where he could find better-suited reference materials and study guides.

Larry studied for another four months and then retook the exam. He passed with flying colors!

So, shop around first. Find what works best for you. And if necessary, consult with other professionals—they may be able to point you in the right direction.

Use the Exam Content Outline

Instead of trying to study at random, use the exam content outline as a guide. It is freely available from PMI. Use this with your reference materials, mock exams, and PMBOK Guide. The exam content outline is excellent because it is a complete syllabus! It will significantly help put all the information you absorb into perspective, making everything easier to understand and process.

Put It in Writing

How long do you plan to study? Write it down by creating a solid schedule you can adhere to. This schedule should include studying the PMBOK Guide, reference materials, and any other material you use. This will keep you from jumping from one source to the next, which may confuse you unless you do so to cross-reference certain parts.

If you want, you can set 15 minutes before you begin your studies to write down important information you have learned, such as project management processes and formulas.

I suggest that you take mock tests after each chapter you study. Determine what you are struggling with, and focus on that until you fully grasp it.

The Importance of Mock Exams

When you create your study plan, make sure you include mock exams. These are a great way to address anything you don't understand. Talk to a project management professional if you don't find clarity in the PMBOK Guide or other material. Let them show and explain the perplexing concepts until you're familiar and comfortable with them. Be sure to take your mock exams in a quiet, undisturbed space.

There's No Shame in Support

Admitting you need support while preparing for the PMP exam

is *not* a sign of weakness. Don't underestimate yourself, but don't overestimate either. So, find another professional to talk to, preferably someone who has already gone through this process. Who would make a better guide than the person who walked the path?

What kind of support would benefit you most? It can be anything, from an online community, a social media support group, a trusted professional colleague, or perhaps a study buddy.

Tackling Your Timeline

You may have all the strategies down for efficient studying, but you'll still be in a dilemma without proper time management. Like with projects, preparing for the PMP exam is bound to a timeframe. But how can you manage your time for optimum results?

Be Optimistic, But Also Realistic

Even if you are optimistically pumped and ready to learn all there is to know, you must also be realistic. What is your current situation? Are you employed full-time or part-time? Are you single or married? Do you have children? What other responsibilities, besides work, do you have? All this must be taken into consideration when planning your timeline.

Naturally, you'll have more time for studying if you have more time. Some ace the PMP exam with only two or three months of studying. Maybe it's the same for you. But, if you have a lot on your plate, you may take up to six months to prepare.

The issue is that if you schedule your exam for a date too soon, you may not be prepared enough to pass the exam. On the other hand, if you study for too long, you may lose interest and focus, and much hard work can go down the drain. Another thing to think about is mock exams using a PMP exam simulator, which can take hours to finish—you'll have to see when you have enough time available and schedule around that.

The same applies to everything else: your responsibilities, work, chores, and family time, among other things. Build your schedule while being nothing but realistic.

Project Management Overload!

You're not a robot. You don't have a little screen that will display: "Warning, project management overload!" You're only human. Allow yourself some breaks, especially if you're a workaholic. Don't tire your mind too much. A fatigued mind cannot focus or remember valuable information. Take a break whenever your mind feels tired. Yes, you should push yourself to a degree—just don't cause an avalanche.

Spotting Opportunities

While I was studying for the PMP exam, there were some aspects relating to a project my then-employer expected me to handle. This meant I had to drive quite a distance daily and work longer hours. I felt frustrated. This whole thing took up a massive chunk of my study time. Plus, I figured I'd have to give up exercising, which I love.

But then, after a long day's work, it dawned on me—I have *more* time to study now than I had before! Why didn't I realize it sooner? Does it make sense?

Let me explain: I got a PDF version of the PMBOK Guide, which I took wherever I went. I found podcasts and audiobooks that I played in my car while driving. The bonus was that I even listened to them while exercising! I then got the bright idea of recording myself while reading the PMBOK Guide to listen to that.

I'll tell you, it helped me a great deal! When I had time to sit quietly and study, I recalled what I listened to. It helped shape my understanding of theories and applications. So, look for opportunities and ways to learn, even if it's not conventional. Listen to audiobooks, podcasts, or your own recorded voice when you stand in a queue, wait for feedback, are stuck in traffic, or are wherever you are.

Stop making excuses. Start coming up with solutions.

Make the Most of It!

You can make the most of your study plan and timeline by applying a few more ideas. As you review your study material, including the PMBOK Guide, highlight keywords and phrases. Be sure not to highlight too much, though. You can either do this when you start your studies or skim through your materials before you start studying.

Next, summarize the highlighted keywords and phrases in a book or digitally on a computer. Use different colors for different areas and so forth. Your brain loves colors and will find it easier to recall learned information.

Once you're done, read everything back to yourself. Even

though it's a summary, everything should still make sense. But don't only use the summaries to learn. Use all study materials and have the summaries remind you of your learning.

Learn from brain charts, pictures, flashcards, mnemonics, and music. Use whatever works for you. Don't be coy! You know yourself best.

Another excellent method is pretending you are a teacher or, better yet, a professor. Pretend you have a class in front of you, and you have to explain project management to them. Your phantom students don't know anything, so you better teach them well! They need all the details, and everything explained. By doing this, you'll understand and remember information more efficiently and be able to identify the things you have trouble with.

Most importantly, you must know when to stop. Bulldozing your way into the exam doesn't make you a good or bright student. Your brain needs rest, as does your body. Study hard, but rest well. When you keep on watering your garden, everything will drown. Water it at intervals but regularly enough, and everything will flourish! Treat your body and brain in the same way.

Now you have a great understanding of how to study, right? In the next chapter, we'll discuss key things you need to know and understand about project management. There's still a whole exciting journey ahead!

CHAPTER 4:

KEYS TO MASTERING

PROJECT EXECUTION

Project execution is hardly the easiest part of the project. But being a skilled project manager, you probably know that already. You and your team may be masterful at project planning, but when it comes to execution, one of the wagon's wheels comes off. This can cause setbacks and influence the deadline, having to spend extra resources and soothe the wrath of the stakeholders.

Not only will understanding how to master project execution help you with future projects, but it will also benefit you in the PMP exam.

Project Integration, Scope, and Schedule Management

Project integration is about aligning the project elements with a specific goal. Project scope involves all the work and elements required to finalize the project successfully, while project schedule management determines the time that would be needed to finalize all different tasks relating to the project. Let's take a deeper look at these three aspects.

Project Integration Management

To achieve successful project outcomes, project management calls for an all-encompassing strategy. At some stage, all projects require integration, which entails harmonizing the different components and directing them toward a unified goal.

Project integration management is the only way to coordinate the numerous project activities, procedures, and stakeholders. This section will describe it, discuss its significance, and review its procedures.

In basic terms, project integration management is your duty as a project manager to coordinate all the components related to a project. This can include handling disputes between various project components, striking trade-offs between conflicting requests, and coordinating resources, stakeholders, tasks, and other project components.

Let's look at an example: You are working on a project and have set a deadline for completion. However, at some point, you realize that the deadline cannot be met. You now have two options: If you spend more than the budget initially allowed, you can finish the project on time or notify the stakeholders that the project deliverables won't be ready by the deadline.

As a project manager, you must now assess the situation and make an informed decision. You have to consider multiple aspects: the project itself, how it relates to your organization, and how the stakeholders relate to your project. A project should never be managed as an isolated undertaking. This is why project integration management is one of the essential knowledge areas in the PMBOK Guide.

A project has many areas to manage simultaneously, including the scope, schedule, resources, stakeholders, risks, changes, quality, and cost. As a project manager, you must clearly understand how these different areas influence one another. For instance, you must know how the risks associated with a project affect the cost and the stakeholders, as well as how it affects the schedule.

Let's say that because of heightened risk, the project deadline must be moved to a later date. At some point, however, one of your most valuable team members *must* go on leave. Their brother is getting married, and they play a crucial part in the ceremony. This is a massive surprise to you, as you had no idea.

If there had been proper project integration management, you would have known about this and would have been able to prepare. Your team members fall under resources, a project element that must be appropriately managed.

Project Scope Management

Every project has an expected outcome: the deliverables. These features or functions must be the final product of a completed project. How do you know what the deliverables are? It's simple—you'll determine this from the project's requirements. The project scope refers to all the work necessary to deliver a service, product, or result with the required features and functions.

Project scope management comprises three processes:

Planning

During the planning process, you and your team will define all the tasks that must be completed for project success.

Controlling and Monitoring

This process focuses on managing scope creep, analyzing and approving or disapproving changes related to the project, and document tracking.

Closing

Once the project is finalized, an audit must be done to compare the actual outcome (or deliverables) to what was required initially.

Project scope management allows you to prioritize the expectations of your client or stakeholders, as you will better understand how to schedule and use time more effectively. This will result in a higher probability that deadlines are met.

Managing the project scope will give you more control to handle issues that may arise. Such issues may include an inefficient budget, clients or stakeholders that keep changing their expectations, failing to meet a project deadline, changing the overall direction of the project halfway through it, or being told that the deliverables are less than what the client or stakeholder expected.

By remaining in the project scope, you, as the project manager, ensure that tasks unrelated to the project's success are avoided. You'll guide your team to focus only on what is necessary for deliverable satisfaction while remaining within budget and the designated timeframe.

It's advisable to have a document that can be referred to relating to the scope. This document can detail each team member's responsibilities, define the project's parameters, and explain procedures to evaluate and approve completed tasks.

Project Schedule Management

Time affects us, whether we're at home or the office. There's a lot of truth in the phrase "time is money," especially regarding projects. The delay of a project, meaning it continues past its deadline, can incur extra costs not only in money as a resource but also manpower. Time in itself is a resource. This is why project schedule management is so important.

Project schedule management is more than simply determining project tasks and their respective timeframes—it's also about managing assigned resources and dependencies.

Project delays can be costly, so schedule management is crucial to the project's success. When you manage the project schedule, you ensure that the project plan is shared with your entire team, the probability of reaching the project goals is increased, you know how the team and the tasks relate to one another, the project work is structured and organized, the project remains on the right path as planned, thorough data is collected for reporting, and critical tasks are not neglected.

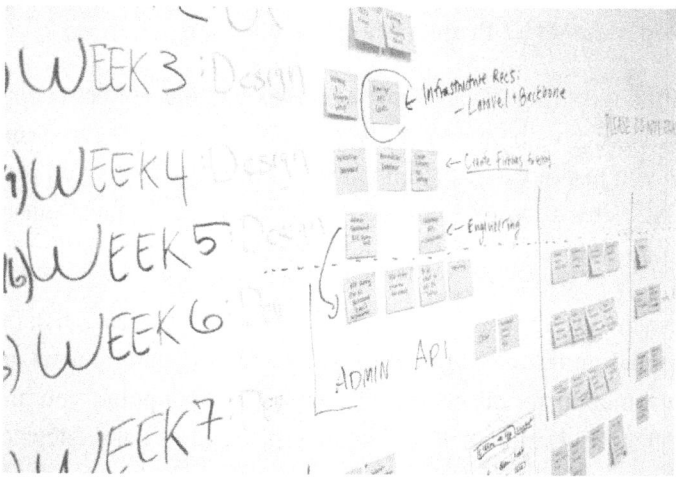

Steps for Successful Project Management

This section will examine the steps required to gain optimum project integration, scope, and schedule management results.

Steps for Project Integration Management Success

Project integration is vital—the glue holds the project together. Therefore, it needs to be managed efficiently. Here, you'll find the steps to gain the best outputs possible.

Step One—The Project Charter

This document is created at the start of every project. It describes the project's budget, processes, timelines, goals, and deliverables. This official document also mentions every stakeholder and critical point of contact. As the project manager, you will use this to navigate through every process and step toward project success.

Step Two—The Project Management Plan

Although the project charter is necessary, the project cannot commence without proper planning. When you go on vacation, do you just buy a map, jump in your car, and go? No, you plan first. Why do you? Because you want to get the most out of your vacation. The same goes for projects.

As you develop the project management plan, you establish the critical milestones, timelines, deliverables, and other vital information for successful evaluation. At this point, you and your team leaders will divide the project into smaller steps or objectives. This will break down the work into more manageable chunks, making managing decisions and risks related to the project more efficient.

Step Three—Project Execution

Now that everything relating to the project is planned per steps one and two, the third step is to implement all of this. The project charter and management plan serve as a guideline for your team to ensure all required tasks are performed according to their allocated timeframes while remaining within budget.

At this stage, you'll notice how all the functions associated with the project are integrated. Working with your team leaders, you'll manage coordination and communication, stakeholder meetings, resources, tasks, updates, and reports. Teamwork will ensure that all tasks performed and resources spent adhere to the service description. Every effort toward the project's success must be efficient and productive.

Step Four—Project Knowledge

As a project manager, you may find that your team's ideas work wonderfully toward project success. On the other hand, some ideas may not pan out as well as you expected after project execution. Some things may need to be tweaked, or perhaps a lot, to complete the task successfully. This affects your project knowledge, which also needs to be managed.

If everything is going according to plan, let your team members know. If not, and some changes need to be made, they must also be informed sooner rather than later. Even if there's new information, it's not bad—such knowledge means the company's intellectual wealth is growing. Exchanging knowledge becomes more valuable and can quickly motivate organizational innovation.

Monitoring and Controlling Project Work

To remain within the original project management plan, every project-related task must be monitored and controlled. You should regularly perform an earned value analysis to evaluate the project budget and schedule. The tasks should comply with the project charter as long as they are controlled and monitored. This is the only way for the project to remain operational.

Integrated Change Control

Any sudden changes in a project can frustrate you, your team, your organization, and the stakeholders. Therefore, project changes should be kept to a minimum. It is for this reason you have a changes control board—they will assess the proposed changes and try to determine alternative solutions. They should be able to assess the impact of a single change on the entire project. The only way to guarantee positive deliverables is by integrating changes with the ongoing tasks of the project.

Closure

The final step follows when the project is finalized and the final product is approved by the client, which concludes the project. It's not as easy as saying, "Okay! We're done!"— several things must be done. For one, as the project manager, you must conduct a formal review of the entire project with your team leaders. By doing this, you will identify the problems, successes, and newly developed strategies that can all assist your future projects.

This means that the closure of the project provides a reference point for future projects and helps everyone on your team understand how project integration management led to the project's success.

Steps for Project Scope Management Success

Every aspect of the project must constantly be in your vision or scope. Overlooking seemingly minute details can result in project failure. Let's look at the steps necessary for scope management success.

Step One—The Scope Management Plan

Planning is separate from any other activities relating to the project. This ensures that the project scope has all the focus and is carefully developed. The project scope and how it will be defined, validated, and controlled are documented during this process.

Step Two—Gathering Requirements

As the project manager, you will communicate with the stakeholders to document the stakeholders' requirements. This process must be done thoroughly—you will determine and document their desired deliverables and what they need and expect throughout every step of the project.

No one likes unpleasant surprises, and the stakeholders even less so. Therefore, documenting their every requirement in depth can help avoid slip-ups and displeased stakeholders, especially when the project is nearing its deadline.

Step Three—Defining the Scope

The project and expected deliverables will be described in total during this process. The scope will explain, in great detail, what the project is supposed to achieve and what it cannot. This will serve as a guide to keep the project in line with the expected goals. Everyone will clearly understand the stakeholders' needs and know what is expected of them regarding project performance.

Step Four—The Work Breakdown Structure (WBS)

Many project managers who ignore this step find out (often too late) just how important it is. The work breakdown structure (WBS) allows you and your team to break the work into smaller, more manageable chunks. These are known as "work packages." By doing this, the WBS provides a detailed list of every task that needs to be performed. The project is ready to deliver once all these work packages are completed.

Step Five—The Validate Scope Process

This process occurs at the end of each project's phases. The customer provides feedback on the work done, and either approves or disapproves. This process continues until the customer is presented with the final project deliverables.

Step Six—The Control Scope

During this process, the project's status is monitored, and changes to the scope are managed. Control scope is applied to these changes whenever the client has additional requirements. However, you must ensure that the project advances within the scope baseline. Only then can the recommended and requested changes and the preventative or corrective actions be processed through the integrated change control process.

Preventing Scope Creep and Maintaining Project Focus

Understanding scope creep and knowing how to effectively deal with it is of utmost importance. You and your team and the stakeholders are two parties involved in the project. Both parties must agree on the tasks relevant to the project that must be completed and which tasks will fall outside of the project scope.

The Causes of Scope Creep

The success of a project doesn't only rely on your skills and expertise but also the input and involvement of the stakeholders. Next, you'll find some red flags that indicate a high possibility of scope creep.

Surprise Customer Expectations

This happens when the stakeholders suddenly expect tasks or deliverables outside the initially agreed project scope. These changes can be detrimental to a project, leading to the need for increased budgets, missed deadlines, financial losses, and unhappy clients.

Uninvolvement of Stakeholders

When stakeholders aren't involved throughout the project processes, they can't give feedback. This can make it challenging to meet their expectations. This lack of feedback and communication can result in your team having to do more work.

Underestimating the Complexity of a Project

Taking on a demanding or challenging project may feel nice, but if you and your team underestimate it, you can easily fall victim to scope creep. A project can be more challenging and take longer to complete than you initially thought. Such projects can derail quickly and harm your client–contractor relationship.

Poor Preparation

A project may appear exciting, but without the proper analysis and planning, your team won't have defined and measurable tasks to work with. Planning a detailed project is the only way to hold yourself and the stakeholders responsible for the necessary tasks and deliverables.

Lack of Experience

When the project manager lacks the necessary experience, it can lead to inconsistent processes, dissatisfied clients, missed deadlines, under-budgeting, or unnecessary work.

Preventing and Handling Scope Creep

The best for the project would be to avoid scope creep. However, with proper planning, you can still handle scope creep, even if it does occur. Let's see how.

Develop a Strong Baseline

Before defining a project scope, you must have a detailed and complete perspective of the project and its components. When you meet with stakeholders, make sure that you thoroughly list all of their requirements.

Set Measurable Milestones

Ensure you set detailed and clear objectives and their respective metrics when developing your project plan. Doing this gives you more control over what is done and its quality.

Manage Your Bill Rate

Even if small changes are introduced (in the form of scope creep), they can harm your bill rate, reducing your earnings. Ensure your bill rate includes all costs for the increased value of deliverables.

Start With a Kick-Off Meeting

Host a kick-off meeting once you have fully developed the project scope. Your team and the stakeholders can review accountability, the part cach person will play, milestones, and when the stakeholders can assess the phases and provide input.

It Takes a Pro to Say No

Stakeholders may come with change requests that will not add value to the project or can be detrimental. You're the expert. Therefore, you can disagree. But, instead of just saying "no," communicate openly with your client. Explain how these suggestions would impact the project and find alternative ways of moving forward.

Should you accept their suggestions unrelated to the current project, you can set them aside as components of a new project—one you can start as soon as the current project is completed.

Have a Backup Plan Ready

A backup plan and your original or project scope will significantly help manage scope creep. Decide who on your team will be most effective for checking and approving requested additions or changes while being able to calculate the cost of additional work and determine how timelines can be extended. This will help avoid awkward future discussions while keeping your earnings in check.

The Critical Path Method (CPM)

The critical path method allows project managers to schedule a project effectively. It focuses on the tasks that require the most time to execute (or complete). Delaying these tasks will delay the project completion date. By using the CPM, you'll be able to identify which tasks take more time and resources than were initially allocated. As this may indicate scope creep, you must act quickly and apply project change management.

Communicate Efficiently

Ultimately, you are responsible for the entirety of a project. Should there be any proposed changes to the project scope, be proactive—set up a meeting with the stakeholders and discuss the changes and how they will affect the project. Considering the timeline, decide with your clients on the way forward.

Agree in Black and White

As a written contract defines everything expected from a project, your team and client will know what to expect. This will significantly help to manage scope creep. Duties, timelines, milestones, and deliverables must be clear for you and your client. Involve all stakeholders in your meetings— this is the only way to ensure no expectations are overlooked.

Add an Option for Extra Work

If the stakeholders come up with additional requests, remind them of the project's original scope. Then, you can give them two options: the project continues as per the guideline of the original scope, or you can add the extra requests at an additional cost. This will call for a straightforward response from the client. You won't have to extend the deadline or incur unnecessary expenses.

So, you can effectively launch the project by combining project integration, scope, and scheduling. Keep your eyes wide open and continually watch for scope creep. Work quickly to resolve hiccups and delays, if present.

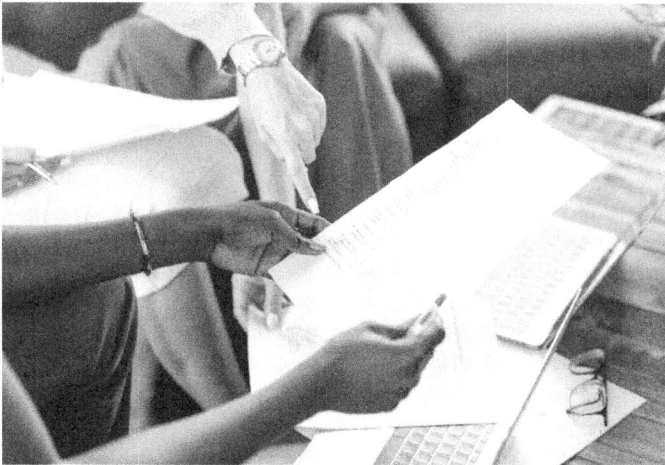

In the next chapter, we'll discuss the subsequent steps for project success: managing the project cost, quality, and resources.

CHAPTER 5:

THE JUGGLER AND

THE GLASS BALL

I've found the perfect illustration and would like to share it with you.

You, the project manager, are like a juggler. You must use your skills to keep cost, quality, and resources in the air. The "cost" and "resource" balls are made of rubber, but the "quality" ball is made of glass.

It makes sense, doesn't it? After all, the client ultimately desires a product or service that signifies quality. This chapter will discuss juggling the three project components without letting the "quality" ball hit the floor.

Project Cost, Quality, and Resource Management

The previous chapter discussed the elements necessary for proper project execution. In this chapter, we'll continue with other vital components of any project that need to be thoroughly managed: cost, quality, and resources.

Project Cost Management

From the start to completion of a project, you must ensure that all expenditures are within budget. You can achieve this through the process of project cost management. It involves estimating, budgeting, and controlling costs in every project's life cycle phase. This is essential for project success.

Why do I say this? A project will only be seen as a success if all work is done according to the requirements and scope, its execution is of high quality, it's completed on or before the deadline, and it's finalized while remaining within the approved budget.

Managing project costs effectively provides a financial baseline to evaluate expenditures and make early adjustments, if necessary, continually.

Let's look at a realistic example. You want a new house, but instead of buying, you want to build one. So, what would be the first concern? That's right—money. How much will it cost? Building the house will need a budget.

You can't randomly conjure up an amount and call it your budget. Several things to consider, such as sub-tasks and other smaller items.

Every aspect of building the house will cost money. To design the house, you'll need an architect. How much does it cost to have the plans approved? Who will you hire to build the house? How many stories do you want the house to be? What kind of materials should they use—standard or high quality? You'll need to consider every expenditure to set up the budget. Only then can you estimate how much this newly built house will cost. That estimation is the budget.

Without a budget, it's impossible to know whether or not you're moving in the right direction, especially after the project has started. Funds must be allocated to every aspect, big and small. If you're working for a large company, you know several projects are probably running at once. And for each project, problems can arise, incurring extra costs.

This is what makes project cost management so vital. With it, both you and the stakeholders know exactly what to expect. With such clarity, you have control over possible scope creep. Project cost management allows you to monitor all processes and intervene quickly. You avoid losing your earnings by maintaining the expected margin and increasing the return on investment (ROI).

Plus, all the data gathered can serve as a guide for future projects, and in the long term, cost trends can be identified.

The Cost of Quality

As a project manager, you *want* to trust that whatever your team members will deliver is nothing but high quality. Ultimately, you just want to pat them on the back and say, "Good job!" Perhaps you have engineers, IT specialists, or other contractors on your team, and you may think it's safe to assume that high quality will be automatically "built" into the project.

I quickly learned that I should never assume that outcomes will always be high quality. Quality is only part of a project if planned, managed, and monitored. This is referred to as "cost of quality (COQ)." It should be part of every project you take on.

Lack of quality in your team's deliverables affects not only your team but also the stakeholders and, ultimately, the customers. By reviewing and managing the COQ, you will get the most from what you invest in quality.

In simple terms, COQ is the total cost needed to identify,

prevent, and deal with flawed deliverables. But don't confuse COQ with the cost of high-grade materials. Yes, high-grade materials can be a part of COQ, but it includes all aspects of the quality of deliverables.

Let's go back to the previous example. As you build your house, you must decide which material to use for the roof. You can use asphalt shingles, as these are cost-effective, or if you want something more pricey, opt for a slated roof.

Because a slated roof is more expensive, it means higher quality, right? Maybe so, but a slated roof is very difficult to install and is excessively heavy. Some houses can't maintain the roof's weight and eventually collapse under the pressure. Also, if 20-30% of the roof is damaged, it is advised that the entire roof is replaced. Yikes!

See, just because something is more expensive doesn't *always* mean it's better. With COQ, you can determine the best materials for your project and how to avoid quality cost issues that may arise later.

The cost of quality is not a process limited to a specific phase of the project. It must be exercised throughout the project's life cycle—from its conception to even beyond the deliverables.

Project Resource Management

You can plan, organize, measure, and manage your team's work with resource management. There are two types of resources: human, which includes a workforce and their particular skills, and nonhuman, such as money, equipment, vehicles, venues, and technology. A resource is anyone or anything you plan to utilize for completing a project. Reusable resources, such as computers, vehicles, or people, are often involved when planning a project.

Also, while managing the resources, you are planning, scheduling, and allocating them to maximize their use and add the most value to the project. You ensure that resources are used on time and remain within budget.

Key Concepts and Processes

While flaws can be cured, prevention is still better. Project execution is only the beginning—the entire project must be managed thoroughly. Projects are fragile. Problems can quickly arise, threatening the budget or quality of the deliverables. You must be ready to overcome these challenges and either prevent or quickly solve incoming problems.

Steps for Project Cost Management

Let's discuss the steps involved in effective cost management. Remember that project cost management isn't only applicable to the execution of the project but is a process that must be followed until its conclusion.

Step One—Project Resource Planning

With your team's help and stakeholders' input, you determine what resources will be necessary for executing and fulfilling the project. This must be done before the project is started. Examining the sub-tasks in the work breakdown structure allows you to identify the resources needed for every project task. These resources can include the number of people and their specific skills, technology and equipment, venues, and materials.

By examining every task in the WBS, you can create a complete inventory of all the resources, which can be used to estimate the project's cost. You can use your knowledge of past projects to identify required resources, but don't hesitate to collaborate. Stakeholders and team members can often provide insightful and valuable input.

You must also determine which resources can only be used for a limited time. This can have a huge effect on cost estimation. During this phase, you must be realistic. For example, you may need a team member with unique expertise. But what if this person is only available for a limited time? Your team members will have to be trained, or you'll have to hire a contractor. Again, this has a significant impact on the project's cost.

Step Two—Cost Estimation

This is estimating the total project cost by considering all the required resources. So, to effectively estimate the project cost, you'll need a detailed list of all the required resources, what each resource will cost, how long they're required, and the timeframe in which they will be available. You'll also need a list of assumptions, details of the potential risks, previous project costs and baselines, and knowledge about your company's financial status and reporting structure.

What makes estimation so tricky is that you must be highly

accurate. The more significant the difference between the estimation and the actual cost, the more likely the project will fail. Thankfully, there are models available to assist with estimations. These models include analogous estimation, parametric modeling, or program evaluation and review technique (PERT).

Step Three—Cost Budgeting

Budgeting involves allocating costs to individual modules or tasks of the project. As issues that can incur additional costs may arise, you must allocate contingency reserves to each task or module. Having a budget is essential, as you now have a cost baseline against which you can evaluate and measure the cost performance of the different phases of the project.

Without the budget, it would be easy to overspend throughout the project's duration, as an estimation would remain an abstract figure. Additionally, this evaluation will clearly show how much of the budget should be released for subsequent tasks and phases.

As you'll likely have a limited financial pool in the initial phases of the project, you must allocate the budget carefully and only to critical tasks and modules. Think about the house that must be built—once you've laid the foundation and built one floor, it will be easier to build the rest. You'll have an idea of what to expect.

Step Four—Cost Control

With cost control, you use the cost baseline to measure cost variances. If this happens, you can correct it immediately by, for example, reducing the scope or allocating more budget to a task. This process must take place throughout the life cycle of the project. It doesn't only involve constant measuring but also prompt and clear-cut reporting.

Managing Cost Overruns

Cost overrun occurs when the cost of a project (or a period or phase) is more than what was budgeted. For example, you have allocated $45,000 of the budget to the first three months of a project, but as you come closer to the end of the third month, you find that the actual cost is $55,000. This is an early sign of possible cost overrun.

You should always try your best to avoid cost overrun, as it harms your earnings and the company's profits. It can also harm your relationship with your clients, causing them to lose trust in your abilities and the project.

Inaccurate estimates often cause cost overruns. There are many things to consider while working on a project estimation: material, people, equipment, and more. Therefore, it can often feel overwhelming. But don't let this tempt you to make random guesses. See if you can find similar projects to yours, then use their estimates and budgets as a"template" to work around. Still, you need to do your homework and create your own estimate.

Find out which similar projects have suffered cost overruns and learn from them. Most importantly, be realistic and informed. Acquire input from various sources, including your team members, stakeholders, company, and other professional project managers.

Continually track your budget and expenses. You can find software to help you with this. As you track material usage, labor, and the progress of tasks, you will quickly notice when your project is in danger of cost overrun. You can remedy it by acting quickly.

Keep your budget transparent. If your team members know how much of the budget is allocated to every task, it will make it easier for them to stick to the budget. You can even provide them with software to help them track budget usage.

Steps for Project Quality Management

Quality does not merely depend on a large enough budget—it relies significantly on the commitment and skills of your team. Let's say your cost estimate is on point, your budget is flawless, and your schedule has been set—what can you do to ensure the deliverables have the quality expected by your clients?

Step One—Use Scale Models

A scale model of the venue you're working at will serve as a visual aid to your team members. With it, they'll quickly identify areas where production bottlenecks can occur and potential hazards and interferences. This will make their work a lot easier. Besides, you don't want an injured or frustrated team member on day two of the project.

Step Two—Be Open to Suggestions

You may just have a highly skilled and experienced member on your team. If this person makes a great suggestion, share it with the rest of the team so everyone can work on it. Remember to give credit where it's due!

Step Three—Be Their Mentor

As the project manager, you must guide your team members, encouraging close interaction. This will help them be cooperative and dedicated to fulfilling the project with quality deliverables.

Step Four—Build Morale

Have you ever seen military units in combat? It's fantastic to see their camaraderie and how close-knit they can be. You are your team's captain—motivate and rile them up to take on the challenge of your project. Make them feel excited and happy to work with you and each other.

Step Five—Determine Their Skills

Get to know your team members and learn about their specific skill sets. Then, designate the tasks or phases of the project they are most skilled in. This will help optimize project progression while ensuring quality deliverables.

Step Six—Communicate

Before the project is executed, inform your team members of the project's quality, professionalism, and budget-related standards. However, communication throughout the project is highly important, as information constantly needs to be shared so everyone, including yourself, will be thoroughly aware of the project's progress and possible challenges.

Quality Control Techniques

As the project aims to yield acceptable quality deliverables, the project process must include quality control techniques. These techniques include statistical sampling, inspections, and control charts. Let's discuss them.

Statistical Sampling

While establishing the project's quality plan, you must decide how frequently samples will be taken of the developing goods or services (the deliverables). These samples are inspected and analyzed to determine their quality. During this process, you can determine whether preventative or corrective measures should be taken to ensure acceptable quality deliverables.

A high rate of quality found while sampling means that the project is progressing well, while a lower rate of quality would mean that measures must be taken and adjustments made to increase the quality of the deliverables.

Inspections

Before the execution of the project, the stakeholders and clients have set their requirements for the quality of deliverables. During inspections, you can observe the progress of the project and compare it to the requirements that were agreed on. This process is also beneficial in identifying risks and addressing them quickly and effectively.

Control Charts

A quality control chart is a handy tool for observing compliance or deviations from the requirements set by clients and stakeholders. It is a graphic that will make it easy to see how progress on the deliverables varies from the customer's specifications and expectations.

The data entered on the chart is gathered through statistical sampling and inspections. Whenever a deviation is found on the chart, your team will have a clear picture of the degree of the deviation. You'll better understand the steps necessary for correcting such a variable.

Forecasting and Handling Resources

Forecasting is the ability of the project manager to predict what the future holds for the project. It does not suggest guessing or being hopeful—these predictions must be based on careful data collection on the project's progress. This data must be thoroughly analyzed before these predictions are made.

A project manager does not take on a project simply because it needs to be done. The client expects deliverables, and not only that, but these deliverables must be of good and acceptable quality.

Gazing Into the Future

Forecasting aims to predict potential outcomes, minimize project risk, and maximize the project's success rate. You'll be able to analyze project risks, determine its likelihood of success, and pinpoint potential areas of improvement. As a project manager, you are well-equipped to foresee resource requirements, project duration, budget, and possible cost overrun.

You'll only be able to use forecasting once sufficient data is available. This is mostly when the project has reached at least 20% of progress. The technique of forecasting you choose must be relevant to the scope and the project's versatility.

Effective Resource Management

The success of a project depends entirely on the required resources. These can include people, materials, and equipment. Every task in every project phase will need resources to be completed. You must be able to successfully schedule resources according to their availability. Lacking the required resources results in resource constraints.

You should already be able to identify possible resource constraints during project planning. Resource constraints can easily throw your project off course, causing poor-quality deliverables.

Resource availability is one of the most important aspects to manage. Let's look at the building of a house again. So, you have bought the most expensive (and top-class) material you could find to build the house's lower floor. But, the contractor you wanted to hire is unavailable and won't be for some time.

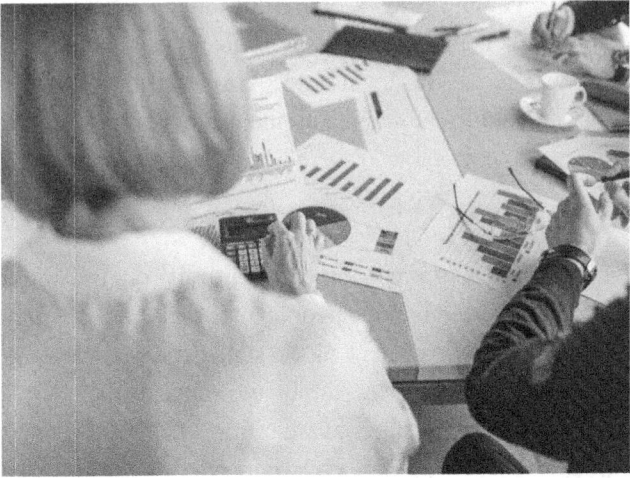

As time is not on your side, you must make do with whoever is available. The only contractor that can help is the one who was supposed to build your swimming pool. They're all too eager to start since it means they'll be paid more.

As their expertise is in building pools, how do you think they'll fare at building the lower level of the house? Their heart is not in it—they just want to get it done to get paid.

How will the quality differ from what you initially expected? Probably a lot! This is why managing resources according to their availability is so vital. It's not all about the cost or quality of the material but the people who will use it.

Now you understand how to ensure the safety of the budget by preventing cost overruns, how to ensure the quality of deliverables, and how to manage resources effectively, you'll sure be able to keep the glass ball from dropping, right?

Your team must work together like a well-oiled machine to strengthen the probability of project success. Communication is key! However, it's vital for your team, and efficient communication is critical between your team and the clients. We'll cover that in the next chapter.

CHAPTER 6:

COMMUNICATIONS AND

PROCUREMENT

Imagine someone is appointed as a football coach, but he never guides or trains his team. He sits on the bench and watches them running around the field. All he does is lose his temper and yell at them whenever they do something he doesn't like. Will they develop? Most likely not. How will they fare against other teams? Probably very poorly. What is missing?

It's about more than just talking. Through effective communication, your team will know what to expect and what is expected of them and understand the project's goals. They will know the limitations and what is allowed. Communication will foster trust, which is necessary for a project to run smoothly and conclude successfully.

Project Communications Management

You'll have to manage communication on how you relay messages and instructions to your team and how they communicate with you and each other. Furthermore, you must also manage any communication with outside entities.

The Dangers of Unmanaged Communication

When communication is not managed, it will negatively impact all responsible parties involved in a project. No one will understand what the project is about or what is expected of them, and you won't be able to delegate tasks according to the individual skill sets of your team members. Additionally, obtaining all the resources required for the project will be virtually impossible. In other words, a lack of communication, or not managing it, will suggest the project is doomed to fail.

Even if there is communication, but the project manager, team members, stakeholders, or clients do not understand what is being communicated, the project will struggle to deliver what was expected. Therefore, communication must exist, be transparent, and be considerate of others. Cutting corners on communication is not worth it—you'll only increase project risks and put your company in danger of massive financial loss.

Developing a Communications Management Plan

Managing communication is about more than being eloquent. According to the PMBOK Guide, "Communication management includes the processes required to ensure timely and appropriate generation, collection, distribution, storage, retrieval and ultimate disposition of project information" ("Communication Management," 2019).

That's a mouthful, I know, but it means all information relating to the project must be communicated clearly and on time. There are several communication types: face-to-face, interactive, push, pull, synchronous, and written.

- **Face-to-face communication** is an in-person meeting with another party, such as a team member or client, to share information.

- **Interactive communication** can be in-person and online, such as through an app that allows direct messaging.

- **Push communication** involves sending information to a large number of people, possibly all parties involved with the project, at the same time. This can be via email or another program or app.

- **Pull communication** is when a person deliberately seeks information by going online or contacting another person to obtain this information.

- **Synchronous communication** allows many people to meet in person or online through a communication platform.

- **Written communication** is when a person writes information down and then passes it or sends it to another person or persons.

Let's explore how to go about developing a communications management plan.

Define How Communication Will Take Place

Inform all the parties involved with the project, such as clients, stakeholders, and team members, which method of communication will be used, how often it will take place, and, if possible, the dates and times of said communications. Remember to include all relevant communication types.

Scheduling Events

Create an effective schedule involving virtual progress status meetings, mandatory planned phone calls, and other digital check-ins.

A List of Essentials

Create a list of everything that must be communicated throughout the project, such as phase updates or progress status.

Assign Reviewers

Several reviews will be required throughout the project. Assign reviewers on time so they know what and when to review.

Be Considerate

If anyone involved with the project has special requests, such as using specific personal pronouns, inform everyone. Also, provide them with pointers on formality and communication etiquette.

Include a Contact Sheet

Provide all the project contributors with a contact sheet that contains details about different collaborators and their delegated tasks and phases. In this way, if someone needs to be contacted urgently about specific tasks, it won't be hard to reach them.

Status Updates

Determine the different status update types, who will be responsible for the updates, and where to locate said updates.

Understanding Project Procurement Management

Let's revisit the illustration of building a house. Anyone who wants a good quality house will pay accordingly, right? Imagine you're paying a substantial amount for the materials, contractors, and laborers. What if you found cracks in the foundation, or they were using second-hand (and slightly damaged) materials? Would you be happy about it? Likely not! Such a house is fated to fall apart.

The same applies to projects. You must apply project procurement management if you want what's best for your project.

Procurement Management Is Paramount

Procurement entails a process where all the materials and services necessary for successful project completion are obtained. If you don't have a clear-cut plan for the resources you'll require for your project, the project will likely take a nose-dive. Procurement management allows you to plan effectively, avoiding expensive errors and ensuring your team obtains the resources and services to close the project successfully.

This will result, in turn, in good quality deliverables. It also helps you find cost-effective materials and services, saving you money and assuring top-notch results. Procurement management will allow you to gather enough information to buy smart. A detailed list of your needs will simplify acquiring these goods or services.

Furthermore, you can negotiate prices with your suppliers. Don't hesitate to do so! See what the best deal is you can get, especially if you require a lot of material from them. The moment you know what you need, begin requesting quotations. Examine them carefully before deciding on a supplier.

The Process of Procurement

Obtaining the resources required for your project is a vital phase in project management. It involves planning, soliciting, and contract administration.

The Procurement Plan

A procurement plan must be developed if your team requires outside resources, such as outsourced services or materials. Remember that you'll have a different relationship and contract for each supplier of the various types of resources. Your team will now begin to prepare requests for proposals (RFPs) and requests for quotes (RFQs). You will also evaluate the opportunities presented by potential partnerships.

An RFQ is all about the price of the resource. Resources such as materials or services are typically available from many suppliers. Usually, the bidder who wins the contract can deliver quality resources and do so per the project schedule at the lowest price.

Although an RFP mentions the price, it is more about meeting the project schedule and resource requirements. As an RFP response, which includes developing a proposal, can be costly for the bidder, your team should not send an RFP to a company that does not qualify to win the bid.

Upon receiving responses to the RFPs and RFQs, your team will evaluate them carefully. After this, the process of awarding and signing contracts will commence. When you obtain the resources from the suppliers, your team can proceed to work on the project. You will then continue with quality and schedule management to ensure the deliverables are acceptable and ready on time.

If there are any contract changes, you will manage them as well. Once the project is concluded, you will work on closing the contracts.

You need to understand the steps described above, as you will need to include this in the project schedule. Each step can take weeks or even months, depending on how complex the project is. The time required for the procurement process can influence the timeframes of other critical tasks, such as whether certain aspects will be performed by the team or outsourced.

Once you know when you will receive the material and

equipment and the completion dates for contracted work, all this must be incorporated into the project schedule. They may need special attention if procurement activities are critical for the project or cause a delay.

Soliciting Bids

Solicitation involves asking bidders the price of their goods or services and supporting information. Usually, solicitation is presented as RFPs or RFQs. Partnerships are built on a case-to-case basis.

But who are these bidders? They are the organizations that can provide the resources, such as goods or services, required to complete the project. In some instances, especially if it is a smaller project, the company your team is doing the project for will have existing suppliers that previously provided resources. Your team should be able to find a performance list of said suppliers.

If no such list exists, your team will develop a list of potential suppliers. From this list, it will be determined which of the suppliers qualify to bid on supplying resources. Eligible bidders must have a schedule of when their resources will be required for the project and when they can start bidding.

A supplier is only eligible if they can supply resources as required by the project and are financially stable. They must be able to supply quality resources and supply these per the project schedule. Your team must also determine if the supplier has the ability and track record to meet deadlines.

Contract Administration

After your team has awarded a contract to the bidder who can add the most value to your project, you or a project representative will meet with the contractor to validate the conditions of the bid and contract.

Less complex contracts, such as for printed materials, only require a reading and signing the contract. This ensures the contractor understands and agrees to the contract terms and project schedule. If a contract is more complex, a meeting must be held with a detailed discussion of the project goals, possible obstacles, the project timeline, schedule, and critical dates, and the processes involved in conflict resolution and improving project processes. Long-lead items or resources that will take a long time to obtain must be addressed early on.

The skills and effort needed to manage a contract depend on the type. The person on your team responsible for managing the contracts will provide the supplier with detailed specifications and ensure that the supplier complies with said specifications. The person managing vendor contracts must ensure that the vendors adhere to the project schedule. They will use the project's requirements as a baseline to track the vendor's performance. They must also provide support and guidance as required by the vendor.

The person who manages partnering arrangements ensures that others remain aligned with the project's goals and processes. As you can see, the skills and effort required for each approach differ considerably.

The contract will contain performance criteria against which the supplier's performance will be evaluated and their contribution to the project's performance. Suppliers are expected to deliver a product or service that adheres to the project schedule and meets quality requirements. Should a contractor not perform according to project expectations, you can use the contract to motivate the supplier to improve their performance or adversely face penalties. Or, you can meet with the supplier to explore innovative ways to improve their performance and comply with project requirements.

Contract management allows you and your team to utilize both approaches. Ultimately, your team can evaluate the situation of non-compliance to determine a way forward. Remember, managing supplier performance is just as crucial to the success of your project as the work performed by your team.

Managing Project Procurement Activities

First, let's discuss the difference between suppliers and vendors. Suppliers typically manufacture products or provide services. Although their products or services may be more expensive, what they offer is usually of higher quality. They often provide raw materials to companies that can help them manufacture products.

Vendors also sell products or services, but generally at a lower price. They also may provide better customer service. Furthermore, if required, vendors can offer customized products or services. Vendors do not offer raw materials but are focused on selling already manufactured products.

Why Choose a Vendor

You may need a product or service that can be purchased but may need maintenance in the long run. This makes the chosen vendor your business partner. Choosing the right vendor means you'll have support and service for as long as you need. The wrong vendor can end up being a significant burden!

Find a vendor by using your project's scope—what exactly do you need, and what do you expect from the vendor? Once you have outlined the project's needs, you can compare vendors. Only look for the resources you genuinely require, or you may spend more than the budget allows or be burdened with products that are useless to the project.

Request a Demo

Many vendors have demo products available. This will help you determine whether a specific product suits your project. All members of your team who will work with the product must learn everything the product has to offer. Better yet, let them test the product to measure its efficiency. Ensure that detailed notes are taken with every demo you are presented with.

Consider the Project's Budget

Remember that with a resource acquired from a vendor, two types of costs may be involved: the immediate cost of purchasing the material or equipment and the future cost of maintaining it. Before choosing a vendor, compare the product's short-term and long-term costs.

Reviews and Recommendations

By now, you should have a good idea of which vendor, product, or service will meet the requirements of your project. But this is not where your investigation ends—it's easy for a vendor to make pretty promises. So, go online and check reviews and recommendations about the vendor. You'll soon be able to tell whether they could deliver quality resources in the past.

Even if a vendor has some negative reviews, don't only focus on that. See if and how they managed to resolve issues with previous clients. Furthermore, there can be no reviews and recommendations if the vendor is new. Don't let that deter you too soon. If possible, give them a chance. Perhaps you'll be able to tell more about them when you meet them or test their demo than you'll learn in reviews.

Now that you know more about communication and procurement, test these theories and put them to use. See what works for your company and projects. Of course, you won't only have to deal with vendors and suppliers but also stakeholders. We'll dive into that in the next chapter.

CHAPTER 7:

THE EYE OF THE STAKEHOLDER

Stakeholders are people who are interested in the outcome of your project, and they can be affected by any point or phase of the project. In the same way, the project can also be affected by their input, which can determine the project's outcome. Communicating throughout the project is essential to ensure project success. Indeed, significance is in the eye of the stakeholder.

Project Stakeholder Management

The requirements of key stakeholders must be met—they have enough influence to either make or break the project. When stakeholders are dissatisfied, a project may be seen as a failure, even if it is completed by the deadline, within budget, and with all the deliverables.

The Importance of Managing Stakeholders

Stakeholders may try to have the most significant influence on your project to gain power. This creates a political environment that, together with the influences of the stakeholders, can pose a risk to the project. Furthermore, the different stakeholders won't share the exact requirements. This can result in stakeholders wanting to influence your project to meet their requirements.

This kind of pressure can bring about changes in the project. Such changes can make the project more complex, affecting project costs and certainty. Still, this does not mean you must see stakeholders in a bad light. You cannot isolate the project because if you do, how will your project yield deliverables that meet *any* requirements?

Remember that your project goal should deliver optimum value for all involved parties. This is what makes project stakeholder management essential—you must be able to find a balance between the involvement of stakeholders and protecting the project from external influences. This is the only way you'll ensure the project's conclusion within the deadline and budget, with deliverables that benefit the stakeholders and their clients.

As long as stakeholders feel they will benefit from a project, they will support it and feel optimistic about doing so. But, if they foresee adverse outcomes, they may want to stop the project or, at the very least, put it in a bad light.

The party that requested the project (the client) often must deal with stakeholders' input. The client must then reconcile the different expectations and requirements of the stakeholders before passing clear directions to the project manager. But, this does not mean stakeholders will then automatically keep their distance. Their involvement must still be managed throughout the project.

Sometimes, decisions are made by a group in an organization rather than one person. This is called a "multiheaded client." Projects sometimes result from endeavors by different development partners or organizations. This is often found in the public sector, for instance, in projects concerning public transport. Projects spearheaded by large organizations or the public sector typically involve many internal and external stakeholders.

Internal Stakeholders

One person may be nominated as the representative of the client organization—this is the person you will be dealing with. The representative must be highly skilled, as they must deal with many organizational stakeholders. They will be subjected to many different influences as they work through and process all the internal stakeholders' requirements.

The representative must negotiate requirements and expectations to successfully convey them to the project manager. The process is more complex because different stakeholders within the organization have different objectives. Still, the representative must find common ground to communicate direction to the project manager.

External Stakeholders

These people are interested in a project but are not part of the client organization. Public sector projects usually have a lot more stakeholders involved than projects for clients in the private sector.

Most Stakeholders Understand Projects

Stakeholders are typically aware that a project is most flexible in its early stages. At this point, most stakeholders will still try to influence the project. The project will begin to pick up momentum as it enters consecutive stages, making it harder to affect change. You'll find that stakeholders will provide less input as a project progresses, and their presence will be felt again strongly when the project is close to concluding.

The project manager must continually manage stakeholder expectations to ensure the project meets their needs. The project manager must also verify that stakeholders are satisfied and feel positive throughout the project phases. Some people are more skilled at managing stakeholders, while others are easier to manage than their counterparts. Publicly funded projects can easily have between 40 and 50 stakeholders involved! They all may have different levels of involvement, requirements, power, and interest. This can make project stakeholder management quite complex!

Things Stakeholders Bring to the Table

Stakeholders aren't meant to make project management a nightmare—they are essential to your projects. In this section, we'll discuss what they bring to your team.

They Offer Experience

Stakeholders often have much experience in projects, products, and services. Therefore, they may be able to offer indispensable expertise. They know how things work in the industry, understand connected processes, and may be able to point out obstacles you haven't considered. They'll also be precise and accurate about the required project deliverables.

They Understand Risks

Stakeholders can provide insights into possible risks as they have experience dealing with them. Keep in mind that risks that are detected early on can be mitigated more easily. Listen to the stakeholders as they raise their concerns and discuss possible risks, especially in the early phases of the project. Knowing and understanding the possible risks will help your team prepare for them and implement contingency plans.

They'll Help Your Project Be Successful

When you understand the requirements and expectations of the stakeholders, you'll have a clear picture and know what to expect yourself. Maintaining communication with them will ensure they are updated on the project's progress, keeping your team and the stakeholders on the same page. When you continue to accept valuable input from stakeholders, their interest in the project may increase, as might their stakes. This greatly boosts the likelihood of your project's success.

Identifying, Engaging, and Managing Stakeholders

As you can see, stakeholder management can be a challenging process. It is crucial to keep key stakeholders satisfied if you'd like to see your project succeed. Let's discuss the processes involved in successful stakeholder management.

The Process of Identifying Stakeholders

The best time to start identifying stakeholders is once the sponsor approves the project charter. Identifying stakeholders includes prioritizing them according to how vested they are in the project and the influence they have on it.

Using the Project Charter

Typically, the project head, influencers, clients, and critical sponsors are named on the project charter. Therefore, this document can help identify stakeholders by providing insights into the involved parties.

Interviewing the Experts and Influencers

You can use the knowledge gained by interviewing the leading influencers and project management experts to determine the key stakeholders.

The Enterprise Environmental Factors

This may include factors such as the organization's structure, industry standards, and competition. Carefully investigating these factors can help you identify the essential stakeholders.

Ask Away!

Find ways to get the stakeholders involved. One great way of doing this is by having brainstorming sessions with your team and experts. Ask many questions and see how they are answered. This will help identify stakeholders. Questions can include the following:

- Who has the power to either accept or reject the project?

- Who are the parties directly or indirectly involved with the project?

- Who are the project's suppliers?

- Who are the project's shareholders?

- Who will benefit from the success of this project?

- Who may be affected by the project's outcome once it is concluded?

Pay close attention to the answers, as they can help determine the key stakeholders.

How to Engage Project Stakeholders

As industries across the globe have become more project than product-oriented, it is essential to keep stakeholders interested in the project. Let's talk about how you can successfully engage them.

Develop a Practical Schedule

The schedule has a different effect on the different stakeholders. As the project manager, you must stick to the schedule to ensure all tasks and phases are completed efficiently and on time. Executives want the project to stay on schedule, as it minimizes their investment risk. Customers want to know a product or service's release date, as they want to take advantage of it as soon as it is available.

When you stay within schedule, it helps everyone perform their tasks on time while expectations are met. This way, the involved parties will want to remain engaged in the project.

Constructive Communication

A project has many different parties involved; therefore, if you want the project to succeed, communication must be constructive. Your team should be able to ask questions whenever they need to. The sponsor will expect budget reports from the resource manager, and customers need to feel that their input matters and that they are well represented.

This is only possible if one group of stakeholders can efficiently communicate with another. Keep the channels of communication open, honest, and productive to strengthen relationships between the different parties.

Goals Must Be Measurable

One way to keep stakeholders interested is by presenting clear goals. Your team's vision of the deliverables should be easily accessed and referenced often. Furthermore, more petite, clear goals or objectives must be set throughout the project.

These smaller goals act as milestones that can continually give everyone involved a sense of achievement. As the successful completion of each milestone is reported to sponsors and executives, they'll have a vivid picture of how the project is progressing.

Keep the Fire Burning

You must be able to positively influence your team members. When you create a work environment everyone can enjoy, it will help increase their productivity. Motivated and driven people can easily affect whoever they come into contact with, thus promoting productivity.

Encourage your team members by being involved—volunteer to give a hand completing tasks, provide them with positive but honest feedback, and lead them by your incredible example. Of course, this means you must be positive and motivated above all.

Addressing Obstacles

You will probably face some difficulties during the project's life cycle. How the stakeholders handle these can have a tremendous effect on the success of the project. When a problem arises, sponsors and executives must be patient while it is resolved.

To keep them cool, you must thoroughly explain why the obstacle appeared and how you plan to deal with it. Process problems effectively, use efficient decision-making, accurate risk analysis, and productive teamwork.

Managing the Project Stakeholders

Even after you've identified and engaged the stakeholders in the project, you still need to manage them. You can achieve this by following the steps discussed in this section.

Know and Understand Them

We've covered how to identify stakeholders earlier in this chapter. This step is essential, as you need to know who they are before you can manage them. Now that you know who they are, you need to understand them. This is achieved by knowing what they expect from you and how your project can benefit from their involvement.

The easiest way to do this is by talking to them. Find out what they expect and need. Furthermore, you need to know if you must engage parties outside of the project that can influence your stakeholders.

Improving Relations

You may need to set objectives to improve relations with your stakeholders. Ask yourself questions such as: *Is the stakeholder satisfied with the progress of the project?* and *Do I have sufficient knowledge of the product or service required?* If not, set new objectives that will help you get there. Seeing the effort from your side can strengthen the relations you and your team have with the stakeholders.

Align Your Strategy With Stakeholder Expectations

If you need to set new objectives to strengthen relations, see how you can interweave these objectives with your current strategies. The stakeholders' expectations must be met. Revising your strategies and adapting them to the new objectives may even be necessary.

Sharing Data

With your strategies in place, you should be able to gather data from the customers who are awaiting the release of the product or service. Share this information with the stakeholders. This will foster trust and transparency, making it easier to deal with stakeholder-related issues. It will also improve the planning around the required resources.

Dive Into Your Data

Stakeholder management doesn't end with developing strategies. While it's a crucial step, you must dive into all the data you can collect. Obtain feedback from internal and external sources. Determine whether your strategies are working well or have room for improvement. Address the issues that cause ineffectiveness in any project area, and revise your strategies if needed.

More Processes for Identifying Stakeholders

Stakeholders should be identified before the project is executed. This means that this process is part of project planning. In this section, we'll discuss two elements of identifying stakeholders: Stakeholder analysis and mapping.

Stakeholder Analysis

This section is similar to what we discussed earlier in the chapter, but we'll look at it more deeply. Here, you'll find the steps for successful stakeholder analysis.

Identify Candidates

List potential stakeholders and how they will relate to the project. Conduct thorough research on each candidate and discover their strengths, how they can be included, and how the project can benefit from their involvement. Narrow the list to those whose profiles fit the project. These candidates must be interested in what you are aiming to achieve.

Prioritize the Stakeholders

Establish each stakeholder's level of resources, interest, passion, and influence on your project. Remember that they must be suitable for their roles—you must be able to use them effectively and productively.

To determine their level of authority regarding the project, each stakeholder must be sorted into one of four groups (Davis, 2023).

Group One: Highly Interested and Highly Resourceful

The candidates falling under this group are potentially your project's greatest assets. You must manage them carefully and effectively, as they should be at your list. You must manage them closely.

Group Two: Highly Interested But Less Resourceful

These candidates may not offer many resources, but don't underestimate them—they're typically very passionate and motivated. They'll happily give the project their everything, using whatever is available to work with. You must keep them informed at all times.

Group Three: Less Interested Yet Highly Resourceful

They have what you need for your project but are not as interested. Do your best to engage them. See that their eyes are fixed on your project and nowhere else. Do not bore them or cause them to become even less interested. They must be kept satisfied throughout the project.

Group Four: Less Interested and Less Resourceful

You may have people who have little interest and few resources to offer. As they are still stakeholders, you should still assign them. Use them to fill project spaces, but designate tasks that fit their profile. You should monitor them throughout the project.

Win Them Over

You must have some control over the stakeholders so your project will move in the right direction. If some need to be motivated or encouraged, meet with them and determine their issues. Try to resolve them while making every effort to win them over.

Threat or Asset?

As the project is progressing, keep tabs on the stakeholders. Determine which of them serve as assets and which are more likely to threaten the project. Deal with those that pose a threat and designate tasks accordingly.

Stakeholder Mapping

Remember the four groups of prioritization? Below is a simple example of stakeholder mapping. It provides a visual matrix to which the different stakeholders can be assigned.

To refresh your memory, these are the four groups as seen in the previous section:

- Highly interested and highly resourceful

- Highly interested but less resourceful

- Less interested yet highly resourceful

- Less interested and less resourceful

Let's say you have four stakeholders who you need to enter into the matrix. Rada Lawless, Ivana Spendalot, Eddie Eagerton, and Rich Reddy are stakeholders. Rada is not very interested in the project nor has resources available. Ivana is showing great interest, and she can provide a lot of resources. Eddie has few resources to offer, but he is excited about the project. Rich Reddy isn't interested, but he has the resources the project needs.

We'll place them in the matrix as follows:

		Keep satisfied	Manage closely
Level of resources	High	Rich Reddy	Ivana Spendalot
	Medium		
	Low	Rada Lawless	Eddie Eagerton
		Monitor	Keep informed
		Low Medium High	
		Level of interest	

There you have it! The example is simple but demonstrates how to use stakeholder mapping. Understanding the importance of the stakeholders in project management is vital for the success of any project. Now, you have the tools to identify stakeholders and keep them engaged. Familiarize yourself with these tools and strategies and use them.

All responsibilities do not fall on the stakeholders, though. As the project manager, you are responsible and accountable for overseeing and managing the entirety of the project. In the next chapter, we'll explore ways you can be responsible with confidence.

CHAPTER 8:

BE RESPONSIBLE

As a project manager, you have a professional and social responsibility. But, instead of dreading this, you must learn to embrace it.

When I started as a project manager, I never could have imagined the levels of responsibility I was given. I felt that I was held accountable for everything and everyone. At times, I wished I could split myself into multiple versions of myself just to give everyone the attention they demanded. I understood the importance of having a clear mind while being held accountable.

But here's the truth—along with your professional and social responsibility, you also have a responsibility toward yourself. Never forget that! Your well-being should be your top priority. If you are focused on doing your best, you will be confident, and all your responsibilities won't feel like a mountain you must conquer. You will realize that you've already conquered it.

Professional and Social Responsibility

For many years, organizations thought financial responsibility should be their priority to maximize shareholder value. However, in recent years, a new notion was adopted that organizations should consider social and environmental concerns and act more responsibly toward society. This is called "corporate social responsibility" (CSR). By working hard and keeping a perspective of the bigger picture, CSR can become part of the goals of most organizations.

The Importance of Corporate Social Responsibility in Project Management

It's not necessarily up to management to get the ball rolling on implementing CSR. You have the opportunity to make CSR part of your projects. This can result in a win-win strategy that benefits both your team (and company) and society. By incorporating CSR, companies accept responsibility for how their activities and projects affect shareholders, customers, employees, communities, and the environment.

An organization should have a positive effect on its neighboring communities. There are four reasons why companies would benefit from integrating CSR into their activities, prioritizing efforts toward social welfare.

Sustainability

Clients' current needs should be met without taking away from future generations. Finding a financial, social, and environmental balance will ensure substantial project progress.

Reputation

When a company makes CSR part of its vision and mission, it can receive more overall support. This means that CSR initiatives have a shining reputation that can improve their image and may even raise the value of their stock. It is better to keep society in mind and be proactive rather than reactive. Many organizations risk their reputation by waiting until issues arise before taking action. CSR will help keep you mindful while working toward avoiding issues and boosting your company's reputation.

Moral Obligation

With the rise of the CSR initiative, many stakeholders will only be gratified when they see that a company strikes a balance between its influence as a business and its social responsibilities.

License to Operate

Many entities, the government included, may only accept contracts if the organization has incorporated CSR in its activities.

What Does CSR Mean for a Project Manager?

As both the organization and the environment must benefit

from CSR-related strategies, you, as a project manager, must also benefit. However, you should not focus solely on how it will benefit your reputation or that of your organization—it goes far beyond that. A company does not simply apply CSR because it is "nice." In today's corporate world, it's a necessity.

Let's discuss some benefits your team and organization can enjoy by incorporating corporate social responsibility.

Client Retention

If the organization you work for is in the business of gaining customers or clients, applying the CSR initiative will significantly benefit you. Clients will notice the organization's consistency and that it shares their values. People are more willing to open their wallets if they believe the business is trustworthy. In simple terms, CSR wins loyalty.

It Provides a Platform to Make a Difference

CSR provides people in the corporate world a platform to make a difference locally and, in many cases, globally. Organizations often have employees who share their organization's vision and mission. They have no issue working toward the same goals in such a case. If your company and your team align their values with CSR, you can all achieve great things and have a significant positive impact.

Read All About It!

By incorporating CSR effectively, you can give your team and organization much-needed exposure. The press loves a good and impactful story. This can create awareness of you and your company's work. However, be genuine about your affinity toward CSR. If people realize your activities are not authentic, your organization can be considered guilty of greenwashing.

Thus, ensure that your mission and values align with the CSR initiative. When your team members believe in your cooperation with CSR, it may fill them with pride. This may motivate them, restore their trust in management, make them more productive, and create a sense of job satisfaction. If you lead your team with truth, press opportunities may follow.

Increase Your Income

Stakeholders want to be sure that a project will result in a positive return on investment. Knowing they will be investing in social purpose will likely win them over more quickly.

Increased Team Engagement

The CSR initiative has a tremendous positive impact on most

employees, resulting in higher employee engagement. This is because CSR gives them a sense of purpose. The same applies to your team members. Most people feel good about giving back to the community—CSR encourages them to be more engaged, especially if your goals align with the initiative.

Attracting and Developing Skills

Did you know that most young people seeking corporate opportunities examine a company's reputation? They are looking for companies that accept and apply the CSR initiative. One way to develop their skills is through social impact. Your team members can develop their skills through an effective volunteer program focusing on individual skill sets. They'll also strengthen their people skills while building their confidence to take on bigger roles in the future.

Ethics and Professional Conduct

We are all familiar with ethical behavior. Picture this: You're in school, there's an important test coming up, and one of your classmates somehow managed to get hold of the question paper. He approaches you and tells you that he wants you to be friends and wants to prove it by giving you the question paper.

The truth is, you have wanted to be friends with this guy for quite some time. Now, you are presented with the opportunity to start a friendship, but it all depends on whether or not you accept this "gift." You're facing an ethical dilemma: If you refuse it, you won't be friends, but if you take it, you're participating in something unethical.

What do you do? If only there was some guide that could help you! Thankfully, in the world of project management, there *is* such a guide!

The Ethical Decision-Making Framework

The PMI introduced the ethical decision-making framework (EDMF) in 2011 to serve as a guide for project managers who need to apply critical thinking when facing an ethical issue (Sao-an, 2021). It is a companion to the PMI Code of Ethics and Professional Conduct. As you are accountable for your team's actions, decisions must be acceptable and ethical and follow PMI standards.

As the EDMF serves as a guide to help make ethical decisions, it presents questions and subquestions, and all are meant to help the project manager recognize ethical issues and eventually make the right decisions and act accordingly. Also, remember that using this framework is solely the responsibility of the person who uses it—so always be honest!

The framework can be used at the beginning of a project before any decisions are made, when a decision needs to be made, or after all decisions have been made. If the EDMF is used for the latter, it can still serve as a guide to reflect and determine if all necessary steps were taken and if all decisions were ethical.

Although the questions are presented chronologically, using the guide will still depend on your project or the ethical issue you are confronting. This may require you to jump back and forth between steps to solve issues effectively. Furthermore, the EDMF is thorough but not all-encompassing. You may encounter ethical problems that fall outside the guide's scope.

Therefore, do not simply use the EDMF to solve all of your ethical issues—instead, be guided and motivated to formulate your own steps and questions to solve issues not covered in the guide.

The EDMF Structure

In this section, we'll look at the structure of the ethical decision-making framework. Examining the steps gives you a clear picture of how it functions.

Step One: Assessment

Don't simply jump to conclusions or make assumptions. Be sure of the facts surrounding the ethical dilemma.

- Is it lawful?

- Is it in agreement with the PMI Code of Ethics and Professional Conduct?

- Is it in alignment with your organization or customer's code of conduct and ethics?

- How does it agree with your ethical values and the community's culture?

If it is unlawful, it would be best to find legal advice. If you find that the answers to the questions hold enough facts to build a strong case, proceed to the next step. If not, do some more digging to find the necessary facts. You can enlist the help of someone you trust if necessary.

Step Two: Alternatives

Take a close look at the situation. Then, consider the options you have.

- Have you thought of different potential choices?

- What are the pros and cons of each alternative choice?

It helps to write down the choices and pros and cons. If the answers to the above questions lead to a satisfactory solution, proceed to the next step. If not, do some more research and see what else you can come up with.

Step Three: Analysis

Determine the choice you'll make and then test its validity.

- Will this decision positively affect or prevent harm to project managers, your employer, stakeholders, clients, the environment, the PMI staff, or future generations?

- Does this choice consider cultural differences?

- Will this look like a good choice when you reflect a year from now?

- Is anyone trying to influence this decision, especially externally?

- Is your mind stress-free and calm?

If your choice positively affects you, you can move on to the next step. If not, take some time to analyze other potential options or review your case.

Step Four: Application

See what happens when you apply ethical principles to your choice.

- Does this decision have the greater good in perspective?

- Does this decision treat others like you want to be treated?

- Will everyone involved benefit from this choice, and is it fair?

You can proceed to the next step if the answer is "yes" to all these questions. Remember, it must be aligned with your values and other ethical principles.

If these questions, or questions of a similar type, cause you to doubt or result in a new ethical issue, rethink your choice, look over the facts, and consider other choices and their implications.

Step Five: Action

In this step, you make your decision.

- Will you accept responsibility for this decision?

- Will you feel good about this decision even if everyone knows about it?

- Are you ready to take action?

If you feel confident and comfortable with your decision, implement it and take action. If not, reverse a few steps until you find a suitable solution.

In the Interest of Stakeholders' Interests

Ethical responsibility affects all walks of life: your job, social life, relationships, clients, stakeholders, the community, the environment, and more. This is why PMI has its Code of Ethics and Professional Conduct in place. Effective management means effectively incorporating ethics into your projects.

Engaging Stakeholders Ethically

A project typically has multiple stakeholders involved. It is the project manager's responsibility to find a balance between all their interests. This can be quite challenging, as the project's deadlines must be met and the deliverables acceptable, all while trying to keep everyone smiling.

Ethics can help a great deal with this. By applying ethical practices, you can see that treating all stakeholders involved is ethical and fair. If a conflict arises among stakeholders, ethics can be used to deal with such conflict quickly and fairly.

The bottom line is that while balancing their interests can be challenging, it is essential for project success. Let's examine some steps you can take to make it somewhat easier.

Never Assume Their Interests or Needs

Some project managers assume what would benefit or interest stakeholders based on their culture or community. You should *never* do this. As an example, think about your closest friends. You're a tight-knit group, right? Still, you do not necessarily share the same interests, nor would the same things benefit you all.

What makes their needs and interests different? Many things shape us, including gender, age, beliefs, and socioeconomic background.

Transparent Targets

Be transparent about your targets and goals throughout the project, especially when decisions must be made. Stakeholders may want to share their insights and suggestions for the betterment of the project.

Set Financial Objectives Without Neglecting Social Responsibility

There is no shame in wanting to increase revenue. Nonetheless, you must always adhere to moral codes. Always be aware of the seriousness of social responsibility and the consideration of environmental factors.

The PMI initiated corporate social responsibility for good reasons. We may be project managers, CEOs, or executives, but ultimately, we're all people. We're emotional beings with thoughts and needs. I love the ethical decision-making framework question that asks if what we do to others is what we want them to do to us. Isn't that the pinnacle of responsibility? The rest will fall into place when we care more about people and the environment.

What a journey, won't you agree? All that is left is to prepare for the PMP exam fully. Calm your mind before moving on. In the next chapter, we'll cover exam preparation strategies and how you can manage your time. We're getting you ready for the big day!

CHAPTER 9:

IT'S ALMOST D-DAY!

No, it's not bad; the heading is just an expression. But I'm sure that in your mind, it *feels* like D-Day. That's why you have to prepare yourself both physically and mentally. Well, let's go further into this chapter so you can change it to V-Day: Victory Day! Okay, I know that was a bit corny. But hey, it's true.

Exam Day Preparation and Strategies

You'll have to begin preparing quite some time before the exam day. You know yourself, your schedule, and your preferences best. As explained in Chapter 3, when you study for too long, you may become bored and lose interest. But, if you don't give yourself enough time to study, you may not be prepared enough to pass. You must find a balance.

Priming Yourself for the PMP Exam

To help you prepare, you can consider using the strategies mentioned below.

Create a Study Plan That Suits You

The three domains the PMP exam questions are centered on are people, process, and business environment. Ensure that you have adequate time to study and review all three domains.

Your only chance of passing the exam is to have an efficient study plan—develop it around your personal needs. Your study time will be significantly influenced by when you plan on taking the exam. As soon as the date is set, you'll have a better idea of your available time to study. Still, other factors must be considered, primarily if you work or have other responsibilities. Nonetheless, you must set aside enough time for studying to be well-prepared.

When searching for training courses and study material, ensure they are official and certified. Furthermore, you know how you learn best—do you prefer to study alone or excel in a classroom? Think about your past experiences and pick the best method for you.

If you are an experienced project manager with many years in the field, don't think you don't need to study for one second to pass the test. Don't see these studies as a burden or a chore—see them as a way to test and increase what you know about project management.

It's Less About Memorizing

Your ability to apply your skills will be tested with real-world scenarios. Those who only memorize the countless terminologies throughout the project management domains struggle when they discover that the exam is more about applying skills and knowledge. Therefore, as you study, focus less on memorizing and more on understanding. Don't try to remember every fact like a parrot—if you know the facts but don't understand them, you won't be able to apply them to real scenarios.

I'm not saying you don't need to recall anything at all. No, you must gain the knowledge. Only make sure you understand all of it. You must know the basics, such as knowledge areas, process groups, and standard formulas, but ensure you know how to apply them in real-life scenarios. For example, you must know critical path analysis as well as schedule and cost management formulas to know how to reduce the duration of a project or calculate the factory, prime, or conversion cost of materials used for a project.

Examine the Exam Content Outline

You have access to the exam content outline on the PMP website. Use it wisely—examine it and understand what you're preparing for.

The PMBOK Guide Is Great, But…

Yes, the PMBOK Guide *is* great, but it is not enough. You won't be sufficiently prepared if the PMBOK Guide is your only study material. It contains a lot of information, but you'll still need more. The PMBOK Guide is invaluable when you create a study plan, though. Use the PMBOK Guide as a reference tool together with your other study materials.

Benefit From Free Exam-Prep Resources

You will find the exam content outline on the PMI website and the PMP Handbook and sample questions. Isn't that awesome? You can use these as a starting point to test your knowledge about the three domains and various subject areas.

Brave Is Not Always the Best

While studying independently is a brave decision, it's not necessarily the best. To pass this exam, you need in-depth knowledge of many subjects. You may have a ton of experience, but some of it may not apply to the exam. Remember, the PMI doesn't necessarily share your perspective.

Wouldn't you like the chance to get answers to your questions, share strategies and experiences, and perhaps even engage in networking? There is a way to do this! Simply enroll in a PMP exam prep course. This certification preparation course allows you to spend time with an experienced instructor who can share practical knowledge about beating the exam.

Make Use of Practice Exams

Find PMI-approved practice exams and spend time studying the resources available to you. This will help clear any doubts you may have. Remember the question types? They include multiple-choice, multiple responses, fill-in-the-blanks, hotspot, and matching.

Enlist the Help of an Online Community

Many PMP communities are available where certified professionals share their exam experiences with candidates. You can find plenty of advice by posting your questions to an online forum. However, since many exam takers only go online to vent their frustrations, beware of any toxic and damaging posts. Only go where you will be uplifted and inspired.

How to Get Ready

Understandably, you'll feel quite nervous on the exam day—who wouldn't? Still, there are strategies that you can implement to make the most of the day.

Mental and Physical Preparation

You may be fully prepared as far as the studies are concerned, but you must also be physically and mentally prepared.

Get Enough Sleep

Your mind needs to be clear and sharp for the exam. When your body feels tired, your mind will struggle to keep calm and focused. Remember, the exam is nearly four hours long, so you must be able to handle that in itself. You'll only be able to do so if you are well-rested. Even if you worry that you haven't studied enough, relax your mind and get to bed. Getting enough sleep is more important, especially the night before the exam.

Enjoy Food That Makes You Feel Good

If you're not already doing this, eat healthy food the day before the exam. Junk food or food with an excess of sugar can cause headaches or cause an upset stomach. Trust me, you don't want this on exam day! If your body suffers from any food-related problem, you'll find it difficult to concentrate for the long exam duration.

But don't attempt the exam on an empty stomach, either. This may cause you to feel dizzy and will impair your ability to focus. Stay hydrated, but not so much that you'll have to keep running to the bathroom during the exam.

Don't Try to Cram Information at the Last Minute

You may have studied well and thoroughly, but you may fear missing something deep down. Just let it go and trust in your ability. Trying to gobble up tons of information on the exam day will only cause anxiety. Stay calm and tell yourself *I've studied well, so I will give it my all and perform at my best*.

Do Not Disturb

Don't allow anything to distract you on the day of the exam. Don't go on social media or read the newspaper. Switch off your phone. Arrange with a trusted colleague to handle emergencies if any should arise. Dress in such a way that the temperature of the exam room won't distract you. Wear multiple layers of clothing to remove some layers if it is too warm.

Tell your loved ones they won't be able to reach you on the day, but only after you've completed the exam. You'll want to contact them directly afterward. After all, you'd want to celebrate!

Packing Everything You'll Need

On the evening before the exam, pack everything you'll need for the exam. This includes your study notes, medication if required, ID, papers, some snacks, and a bottle of water. Call the exam center the day before to confirm what you need to take. If you're using medication, inform the exam center staff.

Be the Early Bird

Do your best to reach the exam center at least an hour before the exam starts. An excellent way to plan this is by traveling to the exam center the week before the exam date. This will give you a good idea of how long it will take you to get there, so you'll know when to leave your house on the day to be on time (an hour before the exam).

All exam centers have a security check, which can take some

time. Being there early means you won't feel anxious or rushed. Plus, you'll have time to review some notes (no cramming, though), have a snack, and sip on your water.

Use Noise-Cancelling Headphones

When entering the exam room, ask for noise-cancelling headphones. Most exam centers have them available to those who want to use them. Some people may finish their exams before you do, so they'll get up and talk to the exam room staff while you're still busy. Wearing the headphones will reduce all possible disturbances around you and help you stay focused.

Brain Dump

Some people use the week before the exam to memorize facts, such as knowledge areas, formulas, and process groups. They then practice writing all this information down within five to six minutes. This serves as a reference they can use throughout the exam. Perhaps you'd like to do the same?

When you contact the exam center, ask them if papers will be available that you can write on. See if you can request it so you know what to expect on the day. If you won't be able to write down your brain dump, keep it in the back of your mind. It will still be helpful during the exam.

Anxiety and Time Management Techniques

Although the exam seems long at 230 minutes, once you're in it, it will feel like it's flying by. This means you'll have to manage your time effectively. Plus, you may feel anxiety gnawing at your mind, which you will also have to deal with. Let's review some strategies you can implement to help with this.

Managing Exam Anxiety

It's highly possible that your anxiety stems from unrealistic fears. You can deal with it through the power of a positive mindset and the strategies we'll discuss here.

Know the Exam Room

If you take the exam at a testing center instead of online, remember that all testing centers are different. This means that it's likely that others who have completed the PMP exam didn't experience it in the way you will. Get information about the testing center, such as their policies and processes. Find information on what will happen the moment you walk in while taking the exam and what happens after the exam.

If you're taking the exam online, ensure you understand the rules of the online proctored format. Take the exam in a place where you are confident you will not be disturbed by things such as pets or deliveries. Do a system check before you take the exam so that it won't cause any delays.

Stay Positive!

Anxiety is fed by worry, which means you'll be focusing on negative thoughts. Furthermore, it will unnecessarily consume your much-needed energy. Consciously decide that you will change your mindset and keep it positive. If you begin to feel overwhelmed, take some deep breaths. Encourage yourself with positive affirmations, such as "I got this!"

Know What to Expect

You have developed a study plan, right? You'll benefit from sticking to it. Make sure that you complete exam simulations more than once. Although you may be a skilled project manager, you must keep the PMI's perspective while answering questions. Ultimately, know and understand what a project manager would do during every project management process.

Overcome Unrealistic Fears

Perhaps you fear that you'll be overcome with anxiety. To help with this, complete mock exams in a similar environment to the one in which you'll be taking the actual exam. Then, tell yourself, *See, it's not that bad. I can do the exam without feeling anxious!*

If you're scared that you'll run out of time, remind yourself that it rarely happens that someone doesn't have enough time to complete the exam.

Maybe you worry that you won't answer a question from PMI's perspective. This is why enrolling in a prep course is so important. They'll train you enough to understand and apply PMI's perspective in the exam.

Master Your Test-Taking Strategies

Tell yourself that the exam is not in control—you are. Be sure that you carefully read every question and that you understand it. Be on the lookout for statements that seem accurate but don't honestly answer the question. You're in control! So, control any frustration you may be feeling and turn it into energy you can use to increase your focus.

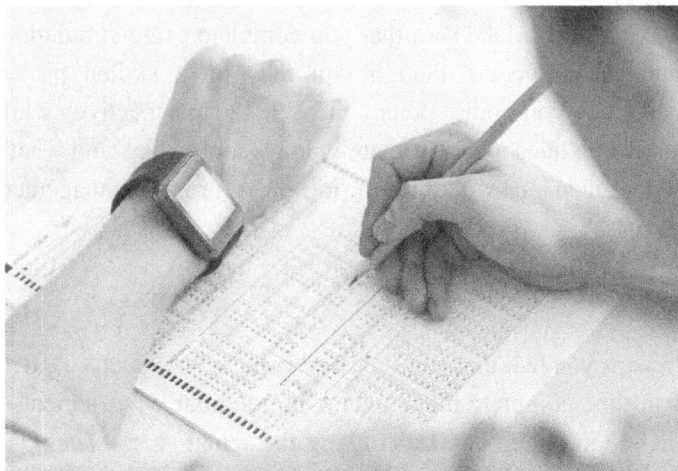

Managing Exam Time

You will have to answer 180 questions within 230 minutes. Therefore, you must enter the exam with a plan to manage your time effectively.

When you calculate the total duration of the exam considering the number of questions, you'll see that you have 1.28 minutes to answer each question. There are three sections of 60 questions each. After each section, you'll be offered a 10-minute break. Some people prefer to keep going without a break, but I strongly advise against it. The exam is quite long, so you need these breaks to refresh your mind.

As you're answering the questions, keep track of the time.

Once you've answered several questions, see how much time and questions you have left. This will give you a clear idea of how much time you can spend on the remaining questions.

Yay! I Know This Answer!

Some questions are more complex than others. If the question is something you know the answer to, answer it immediately. This will help you gain momentum and save time for the trickier questions.

Nope, I Am Stumped

Questions you have no clue about shouldn't be skipped—guess away! These must be questions you are sure you don't know how to answer. Just don't leave any blank spaces.

I'm Having Doubts—I Must Think About This One

The questions you have doubts about, you can mark for review. So, once you've answered all the questions you are sure of, you can go back to answer the more difficult marked questions. You can use the time you spared from quickly answering the more straightforward questions.

However, as mentioned in Chapter 2, once you have completed a section, it is submitted. You can't return to a previous section to answer questions, even if they were marked for review. Therefore, ensure you answer all questions per section before taking a break.

The day is approaching, and my stomach is turning for your sake. Even so, I have confidence in you! You now have all the tools to prepare for the exam. You know what you must do before the day *and* on the day. Use all these tools wisely, and you'll succeed.

Practice questions in the next chapter will prepare you even more. After you've studied some, try some of the questions. I'm sure you'll do great!

CHAPTER 10:

LET'S PRACTICE

How do you feel? If you're feeling nervous, that's okay. Relax, take a few deep breaths, and then attempt the questions in this chapter. The questions are sectioned in their respective domains, covering key knowledge areas and process groups.

You'll find all the answers in the last section. Remember, these examples aim to help you prepare and give you a taste of the actual PMP exam.

Section A: The People Domain

1. The project manager schedules a video conference call to manage scheduling conflicts among virtual and local team members. What is this an example of?

a. It is an example of the smooth/accommodate conflict resolution technique.

b. It is an example of the collaborative/problem-solving conflict resolution technique.

c. It is an example of the force/direct conflict resolution technique.

d. It is an example of the compromise/reconcile conflict resolution technique.

2. While looking at the burndown chart in your Agile project management tool, you discover a lot of work left to do, which will be challenging to complete by the end of the sprint. What action would be best to take?

a. Urgently meet with the team and inform them that they must work overtime to meet the sprint deadline, thereby keeping the client satisfied.

b. Inform the team of the situation by email, encouraging them to put in more effort.

c. Wait for the next stand-up meeting to ask the team why they are working at such a slow pace.

d. Wait for the next retrospective meeting to contemplate what is happening.

3. The project manager must update the project's current schedule and cost information. Which process will be

required?

a. Monitor and control project work.

b. Direct and manage project work

c. Control schedule

d. Control Costs

4. When moving to an Agile working method, companies face a challenge: their need to build teams of "T-shaped" people. What is a "T-shaped" person?

a. A person who specializes in one domain and rarely contributes outside of it.

b. A generalist is willing to take on any work within the backlog, no matter the required skills.

c. Someone who lends their expertise in one area and less-developed skills in associated areas.

d. A person who recently started their career needs coaching from the scrum master.

5. Joyce recently joined a scrum team as a scrum master. She notices that the team is spending too much time refining the product backlog, dramatically affecting their commitment to the sprint work. What should Joyce do to address this issue?

a. She should ask the product owner to take responsibility for refining the product backlog so her development team can focus on their sprint work.

b. She shouldn't do anything since refining the product backlog is essential.

c. She should cancel product backlog refinement meetings, thereby constraining her team to their sprint work.

d. She should coach her team to better manage their time by refining the product backlog for the next sprint while remaining committed to their current sprint.

Section B: The Business Environment Domain

1. Two potential projects are being inspected to choose the one that best aligns with the company's strategic objectives. After considering the limited resources and time constraints, Larry chooses Project X, estimated to generate $100,000 in profit, over Project Y, estimated to generate $150,000 in profit. What is the opportunity cost of Larry's choice?

a. $100,000

b. $150,000

c. −$100,000

d. −$150,000

2. Company XYZ decided to invest $210,000 in a project. In the first year, the project returned a net profit of $14,000. The company had an opportunity to invest $210,000 to earn a 4% return. In this case, what is the economic value added (EVA)?

a. $5,600

b. $196,000

c. $224,000

d. ($5,600)

3. Sarah is managing six projects simultaneously in her organization. Only two projects are similar, while the others are entirely different. Sarah is a _____ in her organization.

a. Portfolio manager

b. Project manager

c. Program Coordinator

d. Program Manager

4. You are appointed as the project manager for a car manufacturing project. You meet with your team and quality head to write the quality management plan. While you're all brainstorming, the quality head points out that the company's perception of the culture is missing. What did you miss referring to?

a. Lessons learned register

b. Lessons learned repositories for similar previous projects

c. Enterprise environmental factors

d. Organizational process assets

5. What are the three factors that can influence the prediction of a project's final cost and schedule outcome?

a. Cost, scope, and schedule

b. Quality of the project plan, actual performance against the plan, management determination

c. Budget, management determination, scope

d. Quality of the project plan, management determination, scope

Section C: The Process Domain

1. Phillip, a stakeholder in an Agile project, attends a planned meeting. He asks the team why this project has no formal documentation. What is their response?

a. The documentation is kept to a bare minimum to respond only to regulatory requirements.

b. Since this is an Agile project, it doesn't require any

documentation since such projects solely focus on delivering added value.

c. Documentation related to Agile projects is only carried out for completed functionalities.

d. Agile needs complicated documentation. Therefore, they are lagging in producing it.

2. Since a project sponsor is risk-averse, he is concerned about the negative impacts on a project. To help with this, the project team identifies four project risks and evaluates their probability of occurrence and their impact if the risks occur. They use a "1-5 scale," with "1" being the lowest and "5" being the highest. The risk probability impact on a table is depicted as A-4 4, B-2 5, C-2 3, and D-3 4. For risk management purposes, in which order should the project manager rank these risks?

a. B, A, D, C

b. B, C, A, D

c. A, D, B, C

d. C, D, A, B

3. You are appointed as the project manager for a large project. Your team just finalized the risk audit process. The project sponsor informs you that the audit process was a complete failure. What did you overlook?

a. An understanding of individual and overall project

risks.

b. Periodically reviewing the risk register and risk report.

c. Defining the risk audit format and effectiveness.

d. Implementing all risk responses and seeking feedback from risk owners.

4. You are the new project manager of the latest technology aircraft project. You joined the project in its initial stages. Your sponsor reassures you that sufficient funds are available for managing this high-profile project. Yet, you are concerned about upcoming threats and believe they can hinder the project's success. What action should you take first?

a. Request management reserve from the sponsor to overcome these threats.

b. Identify and evaluate these upcoming threats.

c. Create risk responses for these upcoming threats.

d. Monitor these upcoming threats and plan accordingly.

5. A project manager directs and manages the project work process, ensuring that the team is completing the work as stipulated in the project management plan to satisfy the objectives and specifications of the project. All the following is executed in the process, except
_____.

a. Implementing changes that have been approved by CCB

b. Setting up a change control system

c. Managing team members and keeping them involved in the project

d. Identifying required changes in the project

Answer Keys for Self-Assessment

Use the answers provided here to assess your knowledge of the domains, process groups, and critical knowledge areas.

Answers to Section A: The People Domain

1. b—The project manager sought to find a solution by scheduling a video call, which is an example of problem-solving and conflict management.

2. c—As their project manager, it is your responsibility to remove the obstacles they may face. As you listen to their updates, you can try to detect the obstacles causing this slow work pace during the ongoing sprint.

3. a—Current cost and schedule information can be updated through the forecasts provided by the monitor and control project work process. This helps stakeholders understand the project's current state, perceive the actions taken to address performance issues, and have a clear picture of the project's future

due to cost and schedule forecasts.

4. c—A "T-shaped" person who specializes in one area but has the skills, flexibility, and mindset for collaboration to help people whenever and wherever necessary.

5. d—With Agile projects, the scrum team works with a gradual elaboration. They only refine the product backlog that they will use in their next sprint or the near future. It is still essential that the team finds a balance between refining the product backlog and focusing on their sprint work.

Answers to Section B: The Business Environment Domain

1. b—The opportunity cost is the value of the missed out or non-selected opportunity or project. Thus, the opportunity cost of selecting Project X over Project Y is $150,000.

2. a—EVA = After Tax Profit: (Capital expenditures x Cost of capital) = $14,000 – ($210,000 x .04) = $5600 as determined by EVA.

3. a—Several related or non-related programs or projects are managed in a coordinated way. Portfolio management is used to bridge the gap between strategy and implementation. It does not focus on one project but considers every project or possible project's potential to achieve the company's goals.

4. c—The plan quality management process is being performed in this situation. Before the meeting, as the project manager, you missed referring to the "Enterprise environmental factors" as it documents cultural perceptions information.

5. b—Various factors can help predict a project's final cost and schedule outcome, such as earned value (EV) and actual cost (AC), but only a few factors can influence factors such as EV and AC. Those factors are the quality of the project plan, actual performance against the plan, and management determination.

Answers to Section C: The Process Domain

1. a—Creating detailed formal documentation is considered a waste of time in Agile projects. The Agile Manifesto states that delivering software that conveys the required value is prioritized over creating documentation. Some documentation is still required therefore, these should be created while considering regulatory requirements or conformance checks when dealing with safety-critical products.

2. c—Probability x Impact provides the risk ranking from highest to lowest. A: 4 x 4 = 16; B: 2 x 5 = 10; C: 2 x 3 = 6; D = 3 x 4 = 12. Therefore, the risks must be ranked A, D, B, and C.

3. c—You missed defining the risk audit format and effectiveness before the audit process, and it caused the risk audit to fail. Tracking describes how risk activities will be recorded and risk management

processes will be audited. Thus, you should have reviewed inputs from the risk management plan, created processes, and defined the audit format to measure the effectiveness before the risk audit process started.

4. b—As the project manager, you should identify and assess upcoming threats that may hinder the project's success first as part of the identify risks process. After identifying the risks, you must assess the risk probabilities and impact as part of the qualitative risk analysis process.

5. b—A change control system is determined and set up during project planning, not during project execution.

How Did It Go?

You can use the results from these sample questions to assess yourself. You can take mock exams, such as in this chapter, at any time during your preparation. The true purpose of the mock tests is to ensure that you are learning and improving. Whenever you attempt mock exams, ensure you'll have the correct answers afterward. It is a lot more effective if you can review your answers, see what you got wrong, and turn your focus to these areas.

If you score at least 80% in your mock exams, you have already increased your chances of passing the actual PMP exam.

Finding Effective Mock Tests

From the myriad of mock tests available today, you must find those that will benefit you. When you look for a suitable and effective mock test, there are some things you must see before you choose to use it:

- There must be various questions covering all the domains and critical knowledge areas.

- Look for ones that offer a full-length practice test.

- The content of the mock test must align with the outline of the actual PMP exam.

- Find mock tests that provide detailed explanations for every answer.

- You should be able to take the mock exam more than just once. It would be great if you could take it multiple times.

This book has provided guidance for preparing, applying for, and taking the exam. You know how complicated the PMP exam will be and have planned accordingly. You have a plan on how to answer the questions, manage your time, and reduce your stress levels.

But, it is equally important to implement this plan even while taking the mock exams. This can help you refine your plan or change it completely until you've developed one that can help you glide through the PMP exam.

You've got this—you're skilled, willing to learn, excited to grow, and ready to conquer!

GET YOUR FREE

AUDIOBOOK NOW!

Unlock instant access to your 'PMP Exam Prep Simplified' audiobook with a quick scan. Your journey toward PMP mastery just got easier - and it's on the house!

Simply point your camera at the QR code above and tap the link that appears to begin your download. Happy studying!

CONCLUSION

If we can liken an organization to a ship, we can see projects as the engine that keeps it moving forward. If the project manager has to manage this "engine," imagine what a tremendously important part they play in helping the organization advance. A multitude of things can go wrong with a ship's engine, and similarly, projects can, and most likely will, face several challenges, too.

The only way to overcome these challenges is by managing them, and that's where the project manager comes in. Managing projects is a huge responsibility. It is a small wonder the PMI has such high standards for a person to become a project management professional.

So, if you're chosen as a candidate, don't be intimidated by how hard the PMP exam is—rather, see it as a compliment and testament to your skills. It's not up to them to prove you have what it takes to become a project-managing professional. It's entirely up to you.

Get all your study materials together, enroll in PMP courses, take plenty of mock exams, and don't forget to use the PMBOK Guide for referencing throughout your journey. Learn to gain knowledge—as much as possible—but focus more on learning to understand. Use the knowledge to become wise.

Remember the three main domains: people, business environment, and process. Learn the different key knowledge areas and process groups and see how they fit within each domain. Once you have developed an effective study plan, stick to it! Don't tire or become bored. Keep reminding yourself that you're doing all this for yourself and your future. Change your mindset if necessary and see all this as an exciting adventure.

Use everything you have learned and will learn. We've discussed many things, such as how vital project integration, the scope of the project, and schedule management are to the successful execution of a project. This also includes monitoring and controlling the project.

Additionally, we covered the management of cost, quality, and resources. You have found methods to improve communication and use them to communicate between team members, stakeholders and more effectively. The procurement processes were explored along with how to identify and engage stakeholders.

We discussed the importance of corporate social responsibility and how its initiation by PMI ensured that organizations would respect the community and environment surrounding every project. We discussed the ethical decision-making framework and how it guides us, as project managers, to be considerate of stakeholders and team members alike.

You now have all the tools and strategies needed to study and prepare for the PMP exam efficiently. As the exam day closes in, you may feel nervous or even a bit anxious. That is entirely understandable. But, nerves or not, when you are thoroughly prepared, you can walk into the exam room with your head held high, confident in your hard work and studies. Remember that even though you have to complete the exam within a specific timeframe, it is still not a race. Use every second you have at your disposal.

Walk in with your plan in place. Put all your strategies into action and finish the exam. You have people waiting to celebrate with you! I'll be there, too, albeit in spirit.

Quiet your pounding heart and hush your racing mind—you can do it! Stand proud and tall and show them all what you've got!

GLOSSARY

- **Agile**: Using Agile software development principles in different management processes, especially product development.

- **Analogous estimation**: A technique a project manager uses to study the variables of previous projects and use that data to deduce the current project's cost and duration.

- **Changes control board (CCB)**: The CCB manages changes to a project's schedule, budget, and scope.

- **Corporate social responsibility (CSR)**: CSR obligates all organizations to accept responsibility for the effect of their activities on employees, shareholders, customers, the community, and the environment.

- **Cost of quality (COQ)**: Allows the company to appraise the quality of its services or products.

- **Deliverables**: The expected and quantifiable services or goods that must be available after a project is completed.

- **Domain**: A group of activities that are related and vital in ensuring positive project outcomes.

- **Earned value analysis (EVA)**: With this, the project manager can calculate the actual amount of project-related work that is done.

- **Enterprise environmental factors (EEF)**: The EEF includes all procedures, policies, legislation, and practices both inside and outside of the organization that will impact the way a project is managed.

- **Ethical decision-making framework (EDMF)**: Serves as a guide to project managers in helping them make decisions when faced with ethical problems.

- **Integration**: A process that brings together different methodologies, systems, and processes to form a united strategy.

- **Key knowledge areas**: The main areas as stipulated by the PMBOK Guide, under which all other processes are grouped according to their type.

- **List of assumptions**: The things a project manager assumes to be true for the project to be completed successfully.

- **Long lead items**: Items that are required for a project but will take a long time to be delivered.

- **Parametric modeling**: The project manager uses existing data to calculate the required resources, time, and cost of completing a project.

- **Process groups**: Enables the project manager to manage and evaluate if all phases are completed to standard, ensuring successful project completion.

- **Program evaluation and review technique (PERT)**: A tool used to identify the tasks, timeframe, and resources required for the completion of a project or one of its phases. It also helps identify potential risks.

- **Project charter**: A document that contains the goals of the project and how it will be of benefit; in other words, it explains why a project is required.

- **Project Management Body of Knowledge (PMBOK) Guide**: Contains all the terminologies, processes, best practices, and guidelines as standard and accepted by PMI.

- **Project Management Institute (PMI)**: An organization focused on advancing other organizations and individuals through guidance, training, and certification.

- **Project management professional (PMP)**: A project manager who has completed the project management examination and has received their certification from PMI.

- **Request for proposal (RFP)**: A company posts an announcement inviting contractors to bid and propose why they would be the best entity to complete a required project.

- **Request for quote (RFQ)**: A company gathers quotations from different contractors and suppliers to obtain the services and resources required to complete a task or project.

- **Return on investment (ROI)**: The profit generated by a project after all expenses made toward its completion have been deducted.

- **Scope**: Includes all the work that needs to be completed to complete a project and defines the functions and features of a product or service.

- **Scope creep**: All the work that is done that is outside of the original project scope. Therefore, it can cause delays and extra costs in concluding the project.

- **Service description**: A detailed description of what an organization, contractor, or project management team can and will offer.

- **Stakeholder**: An individual or organization directly involved in a project. They can be impacted positively or negatively after the project is executed or completed.

- **Work breakdown structure (WBS)**: A tool used to break a large project into smaller and more manageable parts. In this way, the project is divided into many smaller tasks that can be completed more easily.

REFERENCES

Aldena, F. (2018, February 13). *Project procurement management in project management.* ProjectCubicle. https://www.projectcubicle.com/project-procurement-management/

Aldridge, E. (2021a, April 14). *The 10 knowledge areas for project management professionals (PMP).* Project Management Academy. https://projectmanagementacademy.net/resources/blog/understanding-pmp-knowledge-areas-for-the-pmp-exam/

Aldridge, E. (2021b, November 24). *Cost of quality PMP.* Project Management Academy. https://projectmanagementacademy.net/resources/blog/cost-of-quality-pmp/

Baker, E. (2012, October 23). *Planning effective stakeholder management strategies to do the same thing!* Project Management Institute. https://www.pmi.org/learning/library/planning-effective-stakeholder-management-strategies-development-6058

Bhakri, S. (2023, September 5). *PMP exam: Pattern, updates, pass rate, preparation.* Knowledgehut. https://www.knowledgehut.com/blog/project-management/PMP-exam-essential-details

Brannan, L. (2006, November 8). *Project budgeting using the project management knowledge areas*. Project Management Institute. https://www.pmi.org/learning/library/project-budgeting-management-knowledge-areas-8132

Christopher. (2022, September 13). *PMP test questions – PMP sample exam questions and answers*. Brain Sensei. https://brainsensei.com/pmp-test-questions-pmp-sample-exam-questions-answers/?gclid=CjwKCAjwjOunBhB4EiwA94JWsH ltXxARuY8-AS3qkPvQ2NX3A9q_Wnve6W5n7rBqpOLU0kXeG dFLGxoCPa0QAvD_BwE

Communication management. (2019, January 2). Knowledgehut. https://www.knowledgehut.com/tutorials/project-management/communication-management#

Cost management overview. (2023, February 28). GreyCampus. https://www.greycampus.com/opencampus/project-management-professional/cost-management-overview/

Cromwelle, J. (2023, August 2). *25 scientifically proven tips for more effective studying*. MyDegreeGuide. https://www.mydegreeguide.com/how-to-study-tips/#effective-study-skills

Curry, C. (2021, March 24). *5 tips to reduce PMP exam test-taking fear*. RMC Learning Solutions. https://rmcls.com/5-tips-to-reduce-fear-of-taking-pmp-exam/

Dappert, A., & Farquhar, A. (2009). Significance is in the eye of the stakeholder. *Lecture Notes in Computer Science*, 297–308. https://doi.org/10.1007/978-3-642-04346-8_29

Davis, K. D. (2023a, September 5). *PMP certification exam eligibility - A complete checklist*. Knowledgehut. https://www.knowledgehut.com/blog/project-management/pmp-exam-eligibility

Davis, K. D. (2023b, September 5). *Stakeholder analysis: Overview, tools and techniques*. Knowledgehut. https://www.knowledgehut.com/blog/project-management/stakeholder-analysis

Davis, K. D. (2023c, September 5). *Top 60+ PMP exam questions and answers for 2023*. Knowledgehut. https://www.knowledgehut.com/blog/project-management/pmp-exam-questions-and-answers

Edtia. (2022, July 21). *Top 10 tips for passing the PMP exam on the first attempt*. Linkedin. https://www.linkedin.com/pulse/top-10-tips-passing-pmp-exam-first-attempt-edtiasolutions/

EduHubSpot. (2021, January 10). *PMP 2023: New PMP exam prep format: Introduction to PMP (2023) – Video 1* [Video]. YouTube. https://www.youtube.com/watch?v=AXNC_IXwQ_k

Edureka! (2014, August 28). *Project communication management | PMP* [Video]. YouTube. https://www.youtube.com/watch?v=cq0xW4PfiUU

Effective time management: How to manage time during exams? (2022, April 28). Allen Overseas. https://www.allenoverseas.com/blog/effective-time-management-how-to-manage-time-during-exams/

Fichtner, C. (2019, September 13). *Effective PMP study plans from 8 certified project managers*. PM Exam Simulator. https://www.pm-exam-simulator.com/articles/pmp/pmp-study-plan

Fleming, Q. W., & Koppelman, J. M. (1996, January). *Forecasting the final cost and schedule results*. Project Management Institute. https://www.pmi.org/learning/library/earned-value-management-forecasting-cost-schedule-3330

Free top 50+ PMP exam questions and answers for 2023. (2023, July 31). Simplilearn. https://www.simplilearn.com/pmp-sample-questions-and-answers-article

Gabriele, L. A. (2023, April 12). *PMBoK 7 vs. pmbok 6: Evolutions, challenges, and jokes for the modern project manager*. Twproject Blog. https://twproject.com/blog/pmbok-7-vs-pmbok-6-evolutions-challenges-and-jokes-for-the-modern-project-manager/

Gehrig, E. (2018, July 13). *Want to boost your brain power on exam day? Try these 8 simple self-care tips*. Thomas Edison State University. https://blog.tesu.edu/want-to-boost-your-brain-power-on-exam-day-try-these-8-simple-self-care-tips

Gibbs, S. (2015). *Professional and social responsibility PMP prep course – professional responsibility - PMBOK 4 th edition – version 1.0 PMP study group professional and*. Slideplayer. https://slideplayer.com/slide/10489363/

Gummadi, A. (2023, May 2). *The ethics of project management: Balancing stakeholder interests.* Tutorialspoint. https://www.tutorialspoint.com/the-ethics-of-project-management-balancing-stakeholder-interests

How can mock tests increase your chances of passing the PMP certification exam. (2023, January 20). Simplilearn. https://www.simplilearn.com/how-mock-tests-increase-chances-of-passing-pmp-exam-article#self_assessment

How to apply for the PMP exam: Application tips and requirements. (2022, January 19). The Persimmon Group. https://thepersimmongroup.com/how-to-apply-for-the-pmp-exam-application-tips-and-requirements/

How to engage project stakeholders. (2022, June 25). Indeed Career Guide. https://www.indeed.com/career-advice/career-development/engage-project-stakeholders

How to identify and manage project stakeholders? (2022, August 24). Kissflow. https://kissflow.com/project/project-stakeholder-management/

How to manage stakeholders: 10 steps. (2022, June 1). Babington. https://babington.co.uk/insights/help-guidance/how-to-manage-stakeholders-10-steps/

Invensis Learning. (2022, February 18). *Project procurement management | procurement management PMP | PMP training* [Video]. YouTube. https://www.youtube.com/watch?v=gOYNM3lvR9c

Jlancaster86. (2023, March 20). *Why is procurement important to project management?* Oboloo. https://oboloo.com/blog/why-is-procurement-important-to-project-management/

Kelly, B. (2023, April 26). *6 effective communication methods in project management.* Peep Strategy. https://peepstrategy.com/types-of-communication-in-project-management/#google_vignette

Kenton, W. (2021, October 31). *What is a quality control chart and why does it matter?* Investopedia. https://www.investopedia.com/terms/q/quality-control-chart.asp#

Khan, S. A. (2022, February 1). *Six effective tips for PMP exam preparation 2022.* Linkedin. https://www.linkedin.com/pulse/six-effective-tips-pmp-exam-preparation-2022-pmp-pmi-acp-b-eng/

Landau, P. (2021, September 9). *Identifying and overcoming resource constraints in project management.* ProjectManager. https://www.projectmanager.com/blog/resource-constraints-in-project-management

Mathew, K. (2023, February 23). *Overview of PMP exam format.* StarAgile. https://staragile.com/info/project-management/pmp-exam-format#

McLachlan, D. (2022, December 13). *150 PMBOK 7 scenario-based PMP exam questions and answers.* YouTube. https://www.youtube.com/watch?v=Zht0-j03NfQ

Miller, D. (2023, February 24). *The project manager's guide to vendor selection.* ProProfs Project.

https://www.proprofsproject.com/blog/project-manager-guide-to-vendor-selection/

Miller, D., & Oliver, M. (2015, January 1). *Engaging stakeholders for project success*. Project Management Institute. https://www.pmi.org/learning/library/engaging-stakeholders-project-success-11199

Monnappa, A. (2023a, July 18). *Project scope management and its importance in 2023*. Simplilearn. https://www.simplilearn.com/project-scope-management-importance-rar89-article

Monnappa, A. (2023b, July 21). *Top 7 tips for PMP exam preparation*. Simplilearn. https://www.simplilearn.com/tutorials/project-management-tutorial/pmp-exam-prep

Ogunsina, O. (2021, August 3). *10 tips for PMP certification exam success*. Infosec. https://resources.infosecinstitute.com/certifications/pmp/10-tips-for-pmp-certification-exam-success/?gad=1&gclid=CjwKCAjw6eWnBhAKEiwADpnw9vWYsIxGw_mxJmkaDOwn6NY9AS1-DGqggNZmMYi15hsf2Qnxga-8FxoCiDUQAvD_BwE

Patterson, J. L. (1983). *Quality management: The project managers [sic] perspective*. Project Management Institute. https://www.pmi.org/learning/library/quality-management-key-concepts-assurance-5715

PMBOK 7 vs PMBOK 6: Top differences to see. (2023, February 17). Vinsys. https://www.vinsys.com/blog/pmbok-7-vs-pmbok-6/

Project Management Institute. (2017, May). *Project management job growth and talent gap 2017–2027.* https://www.pmi.org/learning/careers/job-growth

Project Management Institute. (2020). *Project management professional (PMP) examination content outline.* https://www.pmi.org/-/media/pmi/documents/public/pdf/certifications/pmp-examination-content-outline.pdf

Project Management Institute. (2021). *PMBOK® Guide.* https://www.pmi.org/pmbok-guide-standards/foundational/pmbok

Project Management Institute. (2023a). *PMP exam preparation.* https://www.pmi.org/certifications/project-management-pmp/pmp-exam-preparation

Project Management Institute. (2023b). *What is PMP certification?* https://www.pmi.org/certifications/project-management-pmp#

Project Management Institute. (2023c). *Why you should get the PMP.* https://www.pmi.org/certifications/project-management-pmp/why-the-pmp#

PMI code of ethics: Importance of ethics in project management. (2023, April 11). Simplilearn. https://www.simplilearn.com/importance-of-ethics-in-project-management-article#

PMI PMP exam actual questions. (2023, August 31). Examtopics. https://www.examtopics.com/exams/pmi/pmp/view/?gclid=CjwKCAjwjOunBhB4EiwA94JWsJe3DLpm0

Gt5uZAVbNjHYyNWOP7LoHurKp-Ec-
A0q_umC2xn-Hl0LhoCNskQAvD_BwE

PMP practice exam. (2023, April 12). PMP Practice Exam.
https://www.pmppracticeexam.org/

PMP preparation resources. (2023, September 7). PMC
Lounge. https://www.pmclounge.com/pmp-
preparation-resources/

PMPwithRay. (2023, January 10). *10 tips to pass the PMP
exam in 2023 | How to prepare for the PMP
certification exam?* [Video]. YouTube.
https://www.youtube.com/watch?v=kiz35B4XG58

Procurement management knowledge area. (2021, August).
PMP Tips. https://www.pm-
exam.com/2021/06/procurement-management-pmp-
study-guide.html

Project cost management: Steps, basics and benefits. (2022,
September 30). EcoSys; Hexagon.
https://www.ecosys.net/knowledge/project-cost-
management/#

Project integration management. (2019). ProjectEngineer.
https://www.projectengineer.net/tutorials/pmp-exam-
tutorial/project-integration-management/

Project management: 5 ways to prevent cost overruns.
(2021). MYOB Australia.
https://www.myob.com/au/enterprise/resources/indus
try-whitepapers/project-management-5-ways-to-
prevent-cost-overruns

Redwall. (2023, March 17). *What Is Project Resource
Management? And Why Bother?* Ganttic.

https://www.ganttic.com/blog/what-is-resource-management#

Rever, H. (2007). *Quality in project management--a practical look at chapter 8 of the PMBOK guide.* Project Management Institute. https://www.pmi.org/learning/library/practice-three-project-quality-management-7198

Rudder, A., & Bottorff, C. (2023, May 5). *Critical path method (CPM): The ultimate guide.* Forbes Advisor. https://www.forbes.com/advisor/business/critical-path-method/#

Sao-an, G. J. (2021, August 5). *PMI ethical decision-making framework (EDMF).* Scribd. https://www.scribd.com/document/482688131/C1b-ETHICS-pdf#

Sawchuck, C. N. (2017, August 3). *Test anxiety: Can it be treated?* Mayo Clinic. https://www.mayoclinic.org/diseases-conditions/generalized-anxiety-disorder/expert-answers/test-anxiety/faq-20058195

Shenoy, S. (2020, June 29). *What to do on your PMP exam day: 9 tips to help you pass.* PM Exam Smartnotes. https://www.pmexamsmartnotes.com/pmp-exam-day-9-tips-to-pass-pmp-exam/

Shivam, J. (2023, February 28). *Professional and social responsibility—ensuring integrity in PMP.* GreyCampus. https://www.greycampus.com/blog/project-management-professional-and-social-responsibility-ensuring-integrity-in-pmp/

Smith, L. W. (2000a, September 7). *Stakeholder analysis: A pivotal practice of successful projects*. Project Management Institute. https://www.pmi.org/learning/library/stakeholder-analysis-pivotal-practice-projects-8905

Smith, L. W. (2000b, September 7). *Stakeholder analysis: A pivotal practice of successful projects*. Project Management Institute. https://www.pmi.org/learning/library/stakeholder-analysis-pivotal-practice-projects-8905

Srivastava, A. (2021, September 6). *PMP exam pattern, changes & PMI triangle*. Project Management Blog. https://projectmanagement.techcanvass.com/pmp-exam-pattern-overview/

Srivastava, A. (2022a, May 10). *PMP exam quiz – people domain*. Project Management Blog. https://projectmanagement.techcanvass.com/pmp-exam-quiz-people-domain/

Srivastava, A. (2022b, May 13). *PMP exam questions [business environment domain]*. Project Management Blog. https://projectmanagement.techcanvass.com/pmp-exam-questions-business-environment/

Srivastava, A. (2022c, May 13). *PMP exam questions [process domain]*. Project Management Blog. https://projectmanagement.techcanvass.com/pmp-exam-questions-process-domain/

Statistical sampling. (2017, December 7). Project Victor. https://projectvictor.com/knowledge-base/statistical-sampling/#

Terrell, M. S. (1999, October). *Project communication management: Five steps*. Project Management Institute. https://www.pmi.org/learning/library/project-communication-management-five-steps-5115

Tharp, J., & Chadhury, P. D. (2008, May 19). *Corporate social responsibility: What it means for the project manager*. Project Management Institute. https://www.pmi.org/learning/library/corporate-social-responsibility-means-project-manager-8368

The Oboloo Team. (2023, March 21). *What's the difference between a supplier and a vendor?* Oboloo. https://oboloo.com/blog/whats-the-difference-between-a-supplier-and-a-vendor/

The Scribe Crew. (2019, May 26). *How to outline your book introduction*. Scribe Media. https://scribemedia.com/write-book-introduction/

The top 7 benefits of having a corporate social responsibility program. (2022, December 1). Benevity. https://benevity.com/resources/corporate-social-responsibility-benefits#

Tom. (2023, August). *Inspections and audits*. Project Management Knowledge. https://project-management-knowledge.com/definitions/i/inspections-and-audits/#

Tristancho, C. (2023, May 10). *Stakeholder mapping 101: A quick guide to stakeholder maps*. ProjectManager. https://www.projectmanager.com/blog/stakeholder-mapping-guide

Turner, R., & Squires, A. (2023, May 17). *An Overview of the PMBOK Guide - SEBoK*. SEBoK. https://sebokwiki.org/wiki/An_Overview_of_the_PM BOK%C2%AE_Guide

van der Walt, D. (2019, July 1). *Strategic corporate social responsibility for projects*. Owner Team Consultation. https://www.ownerteamconsult.com/strategic-corporate-social-responsibility-for-projects/

Verzuh, E. (2005, September 13). *Stakeholder management strategies*. Project Management Institute. https://www.pmi.org/learning/library/stakeholder-management-strategies-applying-risk-management-7479

Vogwell, D. (2003, May 25). *Stakeholder management*. Project Management Institute. https://www.pmi.org/learning/library/stakeholder-management-task-project-success-7736

Waida, M. (2022, April 21). *What is a project communication plan?* Wrike. https://www.wrike.com/blog/what-is-a-project-communication-plan/#

Watt, A. (2014, August 15). *13. procurement management – project management*. Opentextbc. https://opentextbc.ca/projectmanagement/chapter/cha pter-13-procurement-management-project-management/

Welker, B. (2023, September 10). *What is the PMP exam? Everything you need to know to pass*. Crush the PM Exam. https://crushthepmexam.com/what-is-pmp-exam/#

What is a stakeholder in project management? (2022a, August 17). Wrike. https://www.wrike.com/project-management-guide/faq/what-is-a-stakeholder-in-project-management/

What is an ethical decision-making framework? (2023). The Pennsylvania State University. https://aese.psu.edu/teachag/curriculum/modules/bioethics-1/what-is-an-ethical-decision-making-framework

What is forecasting in project management? (n.d.). Wrike. https://www.wrike.com/project-management-guide/faq/what-is-forecasting-in-project-management/

What is PMBOK in project management? (2023, August 23). Wrike. https://www.wrike.com/project-management-guide/faq/what-is-pmbok-in-project-management/

What is project integration management. (2023). Wrike. https://www.wrike.com/project-management-guide/faq/what-is-project-integration-management/

What is project integration management? Explain steps and process. (2023, September 5). Knowledgehut. https://www.knowledgehut.com/blog/project-management/what-is-project-integration-management

What is scope creep and 9 ways to avoid it. (2023, January 26). MBO Partners. https://www.mbopartners.com/blog/how-grow-small-business/6-tips-to-prevent-scope-creep/

What types of questions are on the PMP exam? (2023, January 15). PPC Group. https://www.accidentalpm.online/blog/what-types-of-questions-are-on-the-pmp-exam

Wheeler, E. (2023, May 15). *Introduction to project schedule management*. MIGSO-PCUBED. https://www.migso-pcubed.com/blog/schedule-management/#

White, M. (2018, September 27). *Addressing five key questions to avoid project cost overruns*. EcoSys; Hexagon. https://www.ecosys.net/blog/addressing-five-key-questions-to-avoid-project-cost-overruns/

Zuberi, S. H. (1987). *Contract/Procurement management*. Project Management Institute. https://www.pmi.org/learning/library/contract-procurement-management-9101

REFERENCES:

IMAGES

Barbour, A. (2021). *A person writing on white paper* [Image]. In Pexels. https://www.pexels.com/photo/a-person-writing-on-white-paper-using-pencil-6684265/

Cottonbro Studio. (2020). *White ceramic mug on white paper* [Image]. In Pexels. https://www.pexels.com/photo/white-ceramic-mug-on-white-paper-4778611/

Danilyuk, P. (2021). *Man in black academic gown* [Image]. In Pexels. https://www.pexels.com/photo/photo-of-man-in-black-academic-gown-7944127/

Fortunato, W. (2020). *Coworkers discussing startup project* [Image]. In Pexels. https://www.pexels.com/photo/group-of-multiethnic-coworkers-discussing-startup-project-on-laptops-together-6140676/

Geralt. (2018). *Shaking hands* [Image]. In Pixabay. https://pixabay.com/photos/shaking-hands-handshake-hands-3091906/

Hasanbekava, D. (2021). *Frowning man reading book and taking notes* [Image]. In Pexels. https://www.pexels.com/photo/frowning-man-reading-book-and-taking-notes-in-home-office-7063770/

Jeshoots. (2018). *Woman bites pencil in front of computer* [Image]. In Unsplash. https://unsplash.com/photos/-2vD8lIhdnw

Karpovich, V. (2021). *Woman doing paperwork* [Image]. In Pexels. https://www.pexels.com/photo/woman-doing-paperwork-7433839/

Krukau, Y. (2021). *A man working in an office while wearing a headset* [Image]. In Pexels. https://www.pexels.com/photo/a-man-working-in-an-office-while-wearing-a-headset-8867276/

Mwitt1337. (2017). *Meeting* [Image]. In Pixabay. https://pixabay.com/photos/meeting-business-architect-office-2284501/

NickyPe. (2022). *Glass sphere* [Image]. In Pixabay. https://pixabay.com/photos/glass-sphere-lens-ball-forest-trees-7322496/

Nilov, M. (2021). *Businesswoman talking to her employees* [Image]. In Pexels. https://www.pexels.com/photo/a-businesswoman-talking-to-her-employees-8872173/

Okenka, V. (2017). *Person holding Apple Magic mouse* [Image]. In Pexels. https://www.pexels.com/photo/person-holding-apple-magic-mouse-392018/

14995841. (2020). *Meeting, happy, good news* [Image]. In Pixabay. https://pixabay.com/photos/meeting-happy-good-news-business-4784910/

OpenClipart-Vectors. (2013). *Chart graph diagram* [Image]. In Pixabay. https://pixabay.com/vectors/chart-graph-diagram-line-chart-145231/

Piacquadio, A. (2018a). *Amazed formal male looking at laptop screen* [Image]. In Pexels. https://www.pexels.com/photo/amazed-formal-male-looking-at-laptop-screen-3760809/

Piacquadio, A. (2018b). *Man holding black eyeglasses* [Image]. In Pexels. https://www.pexels.com/photo/photo-of-man-holding-black-eyeglasses-3760137/

Piacquadio, A. (2020). *Cheerful male worker sitting with laptop* [Image]. In Pexels. https://www.pexels.com/photo/cheerful-male-worker-sitting-with-laptop-and-multiethnic-coworkers-3865577/

Startup Stock Photos. (2015). *Blue printer paper on board* [Image]. In Pexels. https://www.pexels.com/photo/blue-printer-paper-7376/

Suhorucov, A. (2020). *Businesswomen checking information in documents* [Image]. In Pexels. https://www.pexels.com/photo/multiethnic-businesswomen-checking-information-in-documents-6457521/